Biographies

IN AMERICAN FOREIGN POLICY

Joseph A. Fry, University of Nevada, Las Vegas
Series Editor

The Biographies in American Foreign Policy Series employs the enduring medium of biography to examine the major episodes and themes in the history of U.S. foreign relations. By viewing policy formation and implementation from the perspective of influential participants, the series seeks to humanize and make more accessible those decisions and events that sometimes appear abstract or distant. Particular attention is devoted to those aspects of the subject's background, personality, and intellect that most influenced his or her approach to U.S. foreign policy, and each individual's role is placed in a context that takes into account domestic affairs, national interests and policies, and international and strategic considerations.

The series is directed primarily at undergraduate and graduate courses in U.S. foreign relations, but it is hoped that the genre and format may also prove attractive to the interested general reader. With these objectives in mind, the length of the volumes has been kept manageable, the documentation has been restricted to direct quotes and particularly controversial assertions, and the bibliographic essays have been tailored to provide historiographical assessment without tedium.

Producing books of high scholarly merit to appeal to a wide range of readers is an ambitious undertaking, and an excellent group of authors has agreed to participate. Some have compiled extensive scholarly records while others are just beginning promising careers, but all are distinguished by their comprehensive knowledge of U.S. foreign relations, their cooperative spirit, and their enthusiasm for the project. It has been a distinct pleasure to have been given the opportunity to work with these scholars as well as with Richard Hopper and his staff at Scholarly Resources.

Volumes Published

Lawrence S. Kaplan, *Thomas Jefferson: Westward the Course of Empire* (1999). Cloth ISBN 0-8420-2629-0   Paper ISBN 0-8420-2630-4

Richard H. Immerman, *John Foster Dulles: Piety, Pragmatism, and Power in U.S. Foreign Policy* (1999). Cloth ISBN 0-8420-2600-2 Paper ISBN 0-8420-2601-0

Thomas W. Zeiler, *Dean Rusk: Defending the American Mission Abroad* (2000). Cloth ISBN 0-8420-2685-1   Paper ISBN 0-8420-2686-X

Edward P. Crapol, *James G. Blaine: Architect of Empire* (2000). Cloth ISBN 0-8420-2604-5   Paper ISBN 0-8420-2605-3

JAMES G.
BLAINE

JAMES G. BLAINE

Architect of Empire

Edward P. Crapol

IN AMERICAN FOREIGN POLICY

Number 4

SR
BOOKS

A Scholarly Resources Inc. Imprint
Wilmington, Delaware

Scholarly Resources Inc.
104 Greenhill Avenue
Wilmington, DE 19805-1897
www.scholarly.com

Library of Congress Cataloging-in-Publication Data

Crapol, Edward P.
    James G. Blaine : architect of empire / Edward P. Crapol.
        p.   cm. — (Biographies in American foreign policy ; no. 4)
    Includes bibliographical references and index.
    ISBN 0-8420-2604-5 (alk. paper). — ISBN 0-8420-2605-3 (pbk. :
alk. paper)
        1. Blaine, James Gillespie, 1830–1893. 2. Cabinet officers—
United States Biography. 3. Politicians—United States Biography.
4. United States—Foreign relations—1865–1898. 5. United
States—Politics and government—1865–1900. 6. Imperialism—
United States—History—19th century. I. Title. II. Series.
E664.B6C83   1999
973.8'6'092—dc21
[B]   99-25105
                                                                                         CIP

⊗ The paper used in this publication meets the minimum requirements of the American National Standard for permanence of paper
for printed library materials, Z39.48, 1984.

For Jeanne

Contents

Acknowledgments

I am indebted to a number of people for their assistance, support, and encouragement along the way, and it is a pleasure to acknowledge their help and aid in writing this book. Tom Terrill, an old friend from graduate school days at the University of Wisconsin in the 1960s, originally introduced me to the fascinating personality and remarkable career of James G. Blaine. When I began this project some three years ago, Tom generously shared his voluminous research notes on Gilded Age politics and late nineteenth-century American foreign relations, for which I am most grateful. I also wish to thank Judy Ewell, a longtime friend and colleague, for her thoughts and insights on the Latin American response to Secretary Blaine's Pan-Americanism. I also benefited from the advice and wisdom of a number of my other colleagues in the History Department at William and Mary, especially Craig Canning, Scott Nelson, Cindy Hahamovitch, Carol Sheriff, and Melvin Ely. Eric Roorda and Beth Murphy, my former undergraduate students who have gone on to become successful and respected young scholars of American foreign relations, provided valuable research assistance and help in locating several key documents. Two of my current graduate students, Kelly Gray and Steve Moore, deserve thanks for their generous aid throughout the project.

I am grateful to Walter LaFeber and Charles Calhoun, both of whom read the entire draft manuscript and provided incisive critical commentary. I am most thankful to Paul Burlin for help with the Maine sources, especially in directing me to the Israel Washburn, Jr., correspondence, and for educating me about other Maine expansionists who accepted and promoted Blaine's imperial agenda. I owe a special debt of gratitude to Tom Coffman, who, through his probing and challenging questions, made me aware of the central importance of James G. Blaine to the sustained, decades-long effort to bring the Hawaiian Islands into the American orbit. Thanks to James Lindgren for research advice and the gift of Edward Stanwood's out-of-print study of Blaine, and to Mary Zeidler, who located and presented me with an original edition of Gail Hamilton's invaluable biography of James G. Blaine. My friend Ed Pease has my gratitude for drafting a map and aiding with the illustrations.

It is a pleasure to thank the general editor of this series, Andy Fry, for his friendship, general equanimity, helpfulness, and superb editing of the manuscript drafts. I also wish to thank Richard Hopper at Scholarly Resources for his unflagging support and encouragement.

I am grateful for the invaluable assistance I received from the staff at the Manuscripts Division, Library of Congress. I also wish to thank the staff at the Maine Historical Society for its friendly advice and professional service. The reference librarians and interlibrary loan staff at William and Mary's Swem Library were always efficient and helpful. Thanks also to Alan Zoellner and his staff in Swem's government documents department. I am indebted to the Franklin D. Roosevelt Library for providing copies of documents from the Sumner Welles Papers, to the Hesburgh Library at University of Notre Dame for material from the Henry O'Connor Papers, and to the Colgate University Library for copies of campaign material on the 1884 election from its Grover Cleveland collection.

I wish to thank my sons, Paul and Andrew, who kindly helped locate illustrations and provided assistance with editing and proofreading chores. I am grateful to my daughters, Heidi and Jennifer, and my sons-in-law, Milam and John, for their moral support and encouragement. Above all, thanks to my wife and best friend, Jeanne Zeidler, whose intelligence, quick wit, and good humor have inspired and sustained me for more than a quarter century.

Preface

"Blaine, Blaine, James G. Blaine, continental liar from the state of Maine." Some variation of this refrain was the immediate and predictable response of my colleagues in the historical profession, along with a few friends and family members, when I told them I was writing a book on James G. Blaine. Occasionally, someone might also recall the taunt used by Democrats in the 1884 presidential campaign, "Regards to Mrs. Fisher. Burn this letter," a reference to Blaine's Mulligan letters, which many believed contained evidence of his dishonesty. These two late nineteenth-century pejorative epigrams, precursors of today's television sound bites, are about all that survive in the nation's collective memory of the man and are recited with the clear implication that Blaine was nothing more than a corrupt and venial Gilded Age spoilsman.

I have not attempted to resolve the issue of Blaine's corruption and dishonesty. His most recent biographer, David S. Muzzey, concluded that the allegations of political corruption were untrue. Certainly, the charges that he engaged in illegal activities were not proven, and James G. Blaine never was convicted of a crime. Another Blaine scholar, R. Hal Williams, has argued that the allegations of corruption stemmed from partisan politics. In 1876 the Maine Republican angered his Democratic opponents in Congress, especially southerners, with his attack on Jefferson Davis and his refusal to support amnesty for the former president of the Confederacy. The Democrats retaliated by accusing Blaine of earlier having used his position as speaker of the House to promote the interests of an Arkansas railroad in which he had been an investor. The charge was false, but Blaine did engage in some questionable business practices, as the Mulligan letters revealed. The taint of political corruption dogged him throughout the remainder of his public career.

This book was written in the hope that it would provide readers with a better understanding of James G. Blaine's pivotal role in shaping late nineteenth-century American foreign relations. Within this study

I aim to explain some of the underlying reasons why the United States acquired an overseas empire at the turn of the century. In my long experience as a college teacher, I have never ceased to be amazed at how woefully ignorant Americans are of their empire and the reasons for its creation. Most Americans, not just college and university students, have little knowledge of the nature and extent of their nation's involvement in world affairs over a century ago. For them, America's global role was of little historical significance prior to 1945, when the United States emerged as a superpower after its victory in World War II. By presenting a study of Blaine's diplomacy, I seek to educate Americans and readers in general about the imperial past of the United States. I believe that the following analysis of James G. Blaine's contributions as one of the chief proponents of America's national destiny and greatness demonstrates that he was the most important late nineteenth-century architect of American empire. His blueprints laid out the design for an imperial structure that was in place at the opening of the twentieth century, and his ideas served as the intellectual groundwork and ideological justification for what became the American Century.

James G. Blaine was America's most able and popular political leader in the late nineteenth century. He and his Gilded Age contemporaries took great pride in their nation's economic, material, and technological progress, and they shared a belief in an American mission to lead the world. Many Americans looked upon Blaine as their foremost statesman, and at the time of his death the often-repeated tribute of his peers was to compare him to Otto von Bismarck and British statesman William E. Gladstone and to claim that what they had been in Europe he had been in the United States. But unlike his European counterparts, Blaine was primarily an architect of empire and not an empire builder. The implementation of his blueprints and the construction of an overseas empire came after his death and were carried out by his many protégés, most notably William McKinley, John Hay, and Elihu Root. Blaine was a transitional figure who, as historian Lester Langley has noted, will be remembered for "articulating an imperial plan but never accomplishing the grand task."

E.P.C.
Williamsburg, Virginia

Chronology

1830

January 31   James G. Blaine is born in West Brownsville, Pennsylvania.

1847

September   Blaine delivers the English salutatory, "The Duty of an Educated American," at the Washington College commencement.

1850

April   Clayton-Bulwer Treaty is signed.
June 30   James G. Blaine marries Harriet Stanwood.

1854

August   Hawaiian annexation treaty is signed; later withdrawn by Hawaiian king, Kamehameha IV.

November   Blaine becomes part owner and coeditor of the *Kennebec Journal*.

1856

June   Blaine attends the first national convention of the Republican Party as a delegate from Maine.

1858

September   Blaine is elected to the lower house of the Maine legislature.

1860

May   Blaine attends Republican national convention in Chicago as supporter of Abraham Lincoln.

November   Lincoln wins election.

1863

January 1	Emancipation Proclamation issued.
November 19	President Lincoln delivers the Gettysburg Address.
December	Blaine enters House of Representatives as member of the 38th Congress from Maine's Kennebec district.

1864

Autumn	Blaine supports Lincoln's reelection to a second term.

1865

April 9	Grant accepts Lee's surrender at Appomattox.
April 14	Lincoln assassinated.
December	Blaine begins second term in House of Representatives.

1867

May–July	Blaine tours Europe with Justin Morrill.

1868

Autumn	Blaine endorses Grant's successful campaign for the presidency.

1869

March 4	Blaine becomes Speaker of the House of Representatives at age thirty-nine.

1870

January	President Grant seeks to annex Santo Domingo.

1871

January	Speaker Blaine informs Grant that he opposes annexation of Santo Domingo.
May 8	Treaty of Washington with Great Britain provides for arbitration of the *Alabama* claims.

1872

March	Speaker Blaine welcomes visiting Japanese delegation led by Lord Iwakura.
November	President Grant wins reelection.

1874

December   Speaker Blaine officially welcomes King Kala-
        kaua and the visiting Hawaiian delegation.

1875

January 30   Reciprocity treaty with Hawaii is signed.

1876

January   Blaine opposes amnesty for Jefferson Davis.
April–June   Mulligan letters episode stigmatizes Blaine as
        corrupt politician.
June   Blaine fails in bid for presidential nomination;
        Rutherford B. Hayes is Republican nominee.
July   Blaine becomes Maine's junior U.S. Senator.

1878

June   Senator Blaine supports federal subsidy for
        steamship line to Brazil.

1879

February   Senator Blaine advocates Chinese exclusion.

1880

November   James A. Garfield wins presidential election.

1881

March 7   Blaine assumes duties as secretary of state in
        the Garfield administration.
July 2   President Garfield is gravely wounded by the
        assassin Charles Guiteau.
September 19 Garfield dies.
September 20 Chester A. Arthur becomes president.
November 22 Secretary Blaine issues invitations to Pan-
        American Congress scheduled to meet in
        Washington, D.C., in 1882.
December 19 Blaine resigns as secretary of state.

1882

January   Secretary of State Frederick Frelinghuysen
        withdraws the invitations to the Pan-American
        Congress.
February   Blaine delivers eulogy to Garfield.

1883

February   Blaine begins sustained lobbying campaign in behalf of a renewal of the Hawaiian reciprocity treaty.

1884

Spring   Volume 1 of Blaine's *Twenty Years of Congress* is published.

June   The Republican Party nominates James G. Blaine as its presidential candidate.

September–   Candidate Blaine stages vigorous campaign
October   against his Democratic opponent, Grover Cleveland.

November   Cleveland narrowly defeats Blaine.

1886

February   Volume 2 of *Twenty Years of Congress* is published. Blaine's two-volume historical work is a popular and financial success.

October   Blaine calls for the United States to overtake Great Britain in the race for empire.

1887

June   Blaine family members embark on an extended tour of Europe.

November   Hawaiian reciprocity treaty renewed with an amendment granting use of Pearl Harbor to the United States.

December   Blaine's "Paris Letter" attacking President Cleveland's tariff message is published.

1888

June   Benjamin Harrison secures the GOP presidential nomination.

August   Blaine returns from Europe and campaigns for Harrison.

November   Harrison defeats Cleveland in presidential election.

1889

March 7	Blaine begins his second appointment as secretary of state.
April	Berlin Conference on Samoa begins.
May–June	Hawaiian king, Kalakaua, resists Secretary Blaine's proposal for an American protectorate over the islands.
June 20	John L. Stevens is appointed U.S. Minister to Hawaii.
October	First International Conference of the American States convenes in Washington, D.C., with Secretary Blaine presiding.

1890

February	Senate ratifies Samoan Treaty with Great Britain and Germany, placing Samoan Islands under joint control of the three powers.
April	First International Conference of the American States establishes the Pan-American Union before adjourning.
May–June	Bering Sea crisis with Great Britain erupts.
October	Congress passes McKinley Tariff with reciprocity provision.

1891

January	King Kalakaua dies; Liliuokalani becomes Queen of the Hawaiian Islands.
June	Temporary *modus vivendi* with Great Britain banning pelagic sealing is signed.
October	Attack on the crew of the *Baltimore* in Valparaiso leads to crisis in Chilean-American relations.

1892

April	Secretary Blaine and Minister Pauncefote sign new *modus vivendi* for arbitration of pelagic sealing issue.
May	Lorrin A. Thurston visits Secretary Blaine and is given "green light" on Hawaiian annexation.
June 4	Blaine resigns as secretary of state.
November	Cleveland defeats Harrison in presidential election.

1893

January 16–17   Hawaiian queen, Liliuokalani, is overthrown
with the support of U.S. Minister John L.
Stevens.

January 27   Blaine dies in Washington, D.C.

1

Years of Preparation

Mr. Blaine comes among us comparatively a stranger. It is but just to say that he is a gentleman of decided talent, of liberal education, extensive travel, and acquainted with the public men and measures of the country.
—*Kennebec Journal*, November 10, 1854

James G. Blaine was born on January 31, 1830, in West Brownsville, Pennsylvania, just south of Pittsburgh, to a comfortably well-to-do family of some social standing and political importance. The tale of his life was not one of log cabin beginnings and rags-to-riches success. As a youth, Blaine enjoyed the advantages afforded by privileged status and independent means, including educational opportunities not generally available to the majority of Americans living in the early republic. His great-grandfather, a prominent businessman and one of the wealthiest men in western Pennsylvania on the eve of the American Revolution, served as George Washington's commissary general of purchases and, family legend has it, relieved the terrible suffering and prevented the total starvation of American troops at Valley Forge. Blaine's grandfather James, for whom he was named, toured Europe as a youth in preparation for a commercial career. In the 1790s this James Blaine held a minor diplomatic post in Washington's administration as special bearer of dispatches. As a young man, Blaine's father, Ephraim Lyon Blaine, also roamed the European countryside and before settling down to raise a family with his attractive bride Maria Gillespie, a woman of some "wealth and society," journeyed to the West Indies and several countries in South America. James G. Blaine may have been raised near the edge of the nation's frontier, but his boyhood heritage was not the hardscrabble struggle for existence that is the stuff of American legend. At the time of Blaine's birth, the family was well established and financially secure, and his immediate fore-bears had been men of distinction who were well traveled, cosmopoli-tan, and worldly wise.

Two things about Blaine's boyhood years stand out. Early on he became an avid reader with a taste for history and literature, fre-quently preferring the solitude of reading to ritual family gatherings and visits from neighborhood friends. He also became fascinated with the rough and tumble of American politics and by his teenage years already was a partisan political junkie. These youthful tendencies be-came distinguishing adult traits. Throughout his life Blaine read and treasured good books, which provided the intellectual foundation for a political career that was launched and enhanced by successes and public acclaim as crusading newspaper editor, accomplished political essayist, and popular historian. After overcoming and shedding his boyhood shyness, Blaine excelled as political stump speaker, a prereq-uisite skill for the successful nineteenth-century politician. As a cam-paigner, Blaine continually amazed his contemporaries, friend and foe alike, with his prodigious memory, never forgetting a name or face even years after having first met the person. Through his reading regi-men, Blaine also accumulated a mental storehouse of facts that he dev-astatingly employed in legislative and political debate.

Young Blaine was fortunate because books and learning were prized in his household. His parents actively fostered and encouraged his education, grooming their son to be a success and to make some-thing of himself in the world. Blaine's formal education began first un-der an English tutor among his relatives, the soon-to-be politically prominent Ewings of Ohio. Then, at the tender age of thirteen, he en-rolled in nearby Washington College, which today is still a fine, small liberal arts institution long since renamed Washington and Jefferson College. Blaine made the most of his opportunities. He was an ambi-tious, hardworking, and precocious student. Graduating at the age of seventeen, he was bestowed the honor of delivering at his college com-mencement in September 1847 the English salutatory on the topic "The Duty of an Educated American."

At the time Blaine gave his salutatory address the United States was at war with Mexico and many Americans believed that their na-tion had the right and duty, or "manifest destiny," to expand through-out the North American continent. In the words of John L. O'Sullivan, editor of the *Democratic Review* and originator of the term "manifest destiny," the United States was "the nation of human progress," and Providence would assure that "the boundless future will be the era of American greatness." Blaine unabashedly accepted this concept of national destiny and greatness, proudly informing his fellow graduates that the "sphere of labor for the educated American is continually enlarging." As proof, he cited the recent annexation of Texas, which brought its vast domain "to our glorious union." Acknowledging that annexation of the Lone Star Republic gave rise to the war that "is now in victorious progress," Blaine anticipated "another great accession of territory—possibly carrying our flag beyond the Great American Desert to the shores of the Pacific sea." If that came to pass, population would follow where armies marched, and the "duty for the scholar is to be continental in extent, and as varied as the demands of a progressive civilization."[1]

It was not too long before this impressionable teenager, obviously caught up in the patriotic fervor of the moment when he gave this ringing endorsement of manifest destiny, changed his position on the unqualified blessings of American territorial expansion. One reason for Blaine's change of heart was his experience as a teacher in the slave state of Kentucky. Taking his own advice about the duty of a scholar to be more continental in outlook, the young man had moved west upon graduation. He accepted a position on the faculty at a boys' academy in Blue Lick Springs, in the heart of the Bluegrass State. The majority of "Professor" Blaine's students were the sons of wealthy planters and slaveholders, and according to one of his earliest biographers, this three-year exposure to the nation's "peculiar institution" helped turn Blaine against slavery. Within a short time after leaving Kentucky, he actively denounced slavery and opposed its further extension into the newly acquired western territories, the Mexican War booty he earlier had so eagerly anticipated.[2]

Probably more important than the Kentucky experience in Blaine's eventual conversion to the antislavery cause was his return to the North, initially to Pennsylvania and finally to Maine, which became his home state and political base for the remainder of his life. After a year or two as a teacher at a school for the blind in Philadelphia and after briefly even toying with the idea of becoming a lawyer, he permanently abandoned his earlier commitment to the "go west" trend of the era. Atypically for a member of his generation, Blaine moved to the nation's easternmost state to seek his fortune in Augusta, Maine, the state capital and hometown of his wife, Harriet Stanwood. In November 1854, at the age of twenty-four, James G. Blaine became part owner and coeditor of the *Kennebec Journal,* a prominent Whig newspaper with a circulation approaching three thousand and a readership that extended to every county of the state.

Blaine's relocation to Maine, in the 1850s a prosperous, bustling state with an economy based on shipping, commerce, and agriculture and with well-established trade links to Asia and the Pacific, proved to be the turning point in his life. At the helm of the *Kennebec Journal* he quickly succeeded, known and respected statewide for his hard-hitting attacks on slavery and the slave power. The weekly grind of reporting and editorializing on the consequences of the Kansas-Nebraska Act or the proposed annexation of Cuba crystallized Blaine's antislavery views. But that was not all. Almost immediately upon his arrival in Maine, Blaine helped create the new Republican party, which was dedicated to free soil and free labor, and to stopping the further expansion of slavery. His organizational talents and charisma on the campaign trail made it clear to all who knew him that James G. Blaine's true calling was politics. His career as a journalist was merely a brief interlude that launched his meteoric rise to political stardom. Within four years after coming to Augusta, Blaine was elected to the Maine legislature; within seven years he was speaker; within nine years he was elected to the U.S. Congress, where in 1869, starting his fourth term and not yet forty years old, he became speaker of the House of Representatives.

Blaine's career path from journalism to politics was not unusual for the time. Unlike today, when electronic media are the public's main news source, it is rare for a print journalist to seek elected office. In the nineteenth century, however, it was more common for reporters and editors working on small-town or regional newspapers to enter politics. For example, in the 1860s and 1870s, during Blaine's tenure in Congress, about 10 percent of his colleagues had started as newspapermen. In the 1990s only a minuscule number of the members of Congress began their careers as print journalists, certainly no more than ten individuals in the House and Senate, which represents just under 2 percent of the total membership. One important reason why more journalists entered politics in Blaine's era was because newspapers and journals were rabidly partisan and highly politicized in those years. Frequently the reward for loyally serving in the trenches on a small-town weekly newspaper as a partisan attack dog was nomination and election to political office. Such was the case with James G. Blaine.

Another reason why newspaper work served as a springboard to public office in this era was the nature of the job. Journalism successfully prepared individuals for politics because being an editor/reporter meant covering most, and frequently all, of the day-to-day tasks of the publishing enterprise. Journalists were generalists and synthesizers, familiar with all of the prominent political issues of the day, and not highly specialized professionals writing exclusively on only one small phase of a contemporary newspaper's total operation, such as local crime, presidential politics, or the Pentagon. Working as an editor on a small-town newspaper during this time was an ideal training ground for politicians because it opened the way for one to become the late nineteenth-century equivalent of today's "policy wonk."

In addition to close coverage of local, state, and national politics, nineteenth-century newspapers carried foreign news on a regular basis and frequently editorialized on world events. The *Kennebec Journal* followed this pattern and as coeditor Blaine received invaluable on-the-job training that rapidly made him a knowledgeable observer of the international scene. Providing regular editorial comment on the foreign policy issues of the day, many of which were the same issues that he would confront a quarter of a century later as secretary of state, gave Blaine a sophisticated grasp of American foreign relations. During these formative years of his intellectual and political development, he acquired not only an internationalist outlook focused on Latin America and Europe but also one that extended to the Pacific Rim and Asia. It was logical and consistent for Blaine to adopt an internationalist approach because it confirmed and complemented his already firmly held sense of American mission—a belief that the United States and the American people should assume a more active role in global affairs and in the improvement of the world.

The first task that Blaine undertook upon assuming the editorial chair of the Augusta newspaper was to read all the old issues of the journal dating back to 1825, the first year of its publication. This exercise in self-education amounted to an intensive crash course in American political history. The founder and original editor of the *Kennebec Journal*, Luther Severance, was a staunch Whig, which meant that his newspaper presented a highly partisan rendition of the politics of the Jacksonian era. Henry Clay, John Quincy Adams, and William H. Seward were the Whig heroes of the era for Severance. Clay had long been a political idol of Blaine's father, and in the 1844 presidential campaign the Blaine household, including fourteen-year-old James, supported the Kentuckian's unsuccessful bid for the White House. Throughout his life, James G. Blaine admired Adams and Seward, but Henry Clay was his foremost political inspiration and model. As a charter member of the Republican party, Blaine adopted the activist government agenda outlined in Clay's "American system," and in the post–Civil War years enthusiastically promoted a protective tariff and federal support for the construction of railroads and other internal improvements.

Luther Severance served as Blaine's first political mentor, strongly influencing the new editor's thinking on American foreign relations and future territorial expansion in the Pacific. In the spring of 1854, six months before Blaine's arrival at the newspaper, a gravely ill Severance returned home to Augusta from Hawaii. Whig President Millard Fillmore had appointed Severance the United States' first commissioner to the Sandwich Islands, as Hawaii was commonly then known, having been so named in 1778 by British explorer Captain James Cook for one of his patrons, John Montague, the Earl of Sandwich. Commissioner Severance easily won the respect and confidence of Hawaii's King Kamehameha III and his council of advisers, many of whom were American missionaries and businessmen. In his discussions with the king and his council the new American representative quickly learned that they feared France had immediate plans to take control of the island kingdom. The best way to counter these imminent French imperial designs, Severance argued to his Hawaiian/American friends, was for the United States to annex the islands.

King Kamehameha and his council were receptive to the idea of American annexation, but Fillmore and his secretary of state, Daniel Webster, were not. In a letter to Webster on March 18, 1851, Severance explained to his chief: "We must not take the islands in virtue of the 'manifest destiny' principle, but can we not accept their voluntary offer? Who has the right to forbid the bans?" Webster replied that the Fillmore administration had no interest in annexing Hawaii and only wished to preserve the independence of the islands. Severance dutifully obeyed Webster's official instructions not to encourage among Hawaiians any hope of annexation, although privately he wrote political friends in Maine recommending such a course of action. To a surprising degree Severance's correspondence bore fruit in his home state. Quite remarkably, Maine in the 1850s became a hotbed of agitation for the annexation of the Sandwich Islands.[3]

One of the first concrete manifestations that Severance's pro-annexation arguments were having some influence upon Maine's political leaders came in January 1854. That month, Israel Washburn, Jr., a Whig representing Maine's Penobscot district, delivered a lengthy speech on the floor of the House of Representatives recommending the annexation of Hawaii. To be sure, Congressman Washburn offered a cautious recommendation that treaded a fine line between Whig expansionism based upon mutual consent and the territorial conquest of empire identified with the Democratic party in its recent war on Mexico. For Washburn, the distinction was crucial. He denounced what he claimed was the Democrats' mindless pursuit of "manifest destiny," and then, somewhat defensively, explained that Maine had a legitimate interest in Hawaiian annexation, "as the largest ship-building and one of the most important commercial States in the Union." But annexation should only come, Washburn emphasized, with the consent of the Hawaiian people.[4]

The *Kennebec Journal* also responded to the case being made for annexation by its original editor. The paper extended its news coverage of events in the Sandwich Islands and proudly announced, prematurely as it turned out, in an editorial: "Make way for these Islands, for they are coming." When Luther Severance returned to Maine in early 1854, the editors hired him on as an occasional guest columnist. For many Whigs and future Republicans throughout the North, Severance's word quickly became gospel on the pros and cons of annexing Hawaii. Blaine was no exception. He, too, was infected by the Hawaiian annexation fever of the 1850s, and much like malaria, it reappeared throughout his life. In the first issue published under his editorship, the *Journal* reprinted an article from a *New York Tribune* correspondent in Honolulu who reported that "annexation seems just now to be coming on apace, and right glad am I that it is so." The drumbeat for annexation continued in the pages of the *Journal* for several months, until news of the death of Kamehameha III in December 1854 reached the mainland early the following year and dashed all hopes for the quick annexation of the islands.[5]

Blaine and his new partner and coeditor at the *Kennebec Journal*, John L. Stevens, another son of Maine who would play an important role in the 1890s effort to bring Hawaii into the Union, were restrained, almost philosophical, in their disappointment over the collapse of the annexationist effort in 1855. In their announcement of the king's death to the *Journal*'s readers, they explained that the new king, Kamehameha IV, seemed "very much disposed to enjoy his regal honors" and did not wish to become a mere citizen in a republic. They pointed out that Californians, who were among those in the forefront of the annexationist movement, were taking a "cool and reasonable view of the subject." Quoting approvingly from editorials in San Francisco newspapers, Blaine and Stevens agreed with one paper's assessment that the annexation "scheme is dead, at least for the present." But the Californians remained optimistic, as did the Maine editors, that the Hawaiian Islands would join the Union in the not-too-distant future.[6]

Another complicating factor for Republicans was that the Democrat Franklin Pierce had been elected in 1852 and his pro-slavery administration actively sought annexation. The entire process was now tainted for Blaine because he feared that the Democrats hoped to annex Hawaii as a territory in order to establish slavery in the islands. That in turn would increase the power of the slave states in the federal government and expand the tentacles of what abolitionists commonly referred to as the slave power. As Blaine's predecessor, Joseph Baker, anticipated in September 1854, the Hawaiians "have never tolerated slavery and therefore, will come in as a Free State, and will add one more to the un-dimmed stars which make up our glorious galaxy." However, after the death of Kamehameha III and with him the treaty that stipulated Hawaii would only agree to be annexed as a full-fledged state in the Union, Blaine and Stevens thought it safer to wait for another opportunity, rather than to risk the chance that Hawaii would become a slave state.[7]

Many northerners, not just Blaine and his coeditor, feared that the expansion of slavery into overseas territories, such as Hawaii in the Pacific or Cuba in the Caribbean, would dangerously escalate section-alism and ultimately threaten the Union. The controversial Kansas-Nebraska Act, more than any other legislation approved by Congress and signed by the president in the 1850s, fueled these northern ap-prehensions. This legislation opened the territories of Kansas and Ne-braska to slavery and was, at least in the eyes of many citizens in the free states, a betrayal of an earlier sectional agreement, the Missouri Compromise of 1820, which had prohibited slavery in these territories. Even more alarming to Blaine and others who were in the vanguard of the newly formed Republican party, the Kansas-Nebraska Act ap-peared to embolden southern expansionists to intensify their efforts to annex Cuba, which, unlike Hawaii, had an existing system of slavery.

Again, the Pierce administration and its pro-slavery allies in Con-gress were identified as the main culprits by the Republican press. In his inaugural address, President Pierce had boldly announced his ex-pansionist agenda with the declaration that "the policy of my Admin-istration will not be controlled by any timid forebodings of evil from expansion." True to his word, Pierce, with the aid of his secretary of state, William Marcy, vigorously sought to annex Hawaii and Cuba, but the Hawaiian effort failed. The scheme to acquire Cuba failed as well, although not before arousing deep suspicions among the Ameri-can public that the "brigand" diplomacy of the administration was to-tally subservient to the interests of slavery and the slave power.[8]

President Pierce's Cuban policy earned the "brigand" label be-cause of a secret diplomatic dispatch, which quickly became known publicly as the Ostend Manifesto, sent to the secretary of state in No-vember 1854 from Ostend, Belgium, by the American ministers to Great Britain, France, and Spain. In this alleged "manifesto" the three ministers recommended "wresting," or in essence stealing, Cuba from Spain if that nation refused to sell its Caribbean colony to the United

States. Secretary Marcy immediately repudiated this recommendation, but the administration's opponents, including Horace Greeley's *New York Tribune* and Blaine's *Kennebec Journal*, would not let the issue die. Republican editors incessantly denounced the manifesto as the diplomacy of unprincipled fortune-hunters, and repeatedly charged that the Pierce administration "has brought disgrace on us abroad." Not wishing to abandon such a handy issue on which to hammer the Democrats, the 1856 Republican platform rejected the manifesto as nothing but the plea of the highwayman that "might makes right," which "was in every respect unworthy of American diplomacy." One of the delegates to the 1856 convention that nominated John C. Fremont for the presidency and adopted the platform decrying Pierce's Cuban policy was James G. Blaine.[9]

In 1856 the Democrats, undaunted by what they viewed as the self-righteous and overly moralistic criticism of Pierce's diplomacy by their Republican rivals, nominated the expansionist James Buchanan and included a plank in their platform insuring "our ascendancy in the Gulf of Mexico," which all understood to mean the annexation of Cuba. After his victory over Fremont, Buchanan sustained the Democratic drive to acquire Cuba. In his 1858 annual message, the president requested funds as an advance payment to Spain in the likelihood that Madrid might be willing to sell Cuba sometime in the immediate future. John Slidell, a pro-slavery senator from Louisiana, became Buchanan's mouthpiece in Congress for this measure, and in early 1859 he recommended a legislative appropriation of $30 million to begin negotiations with Spain. The Slidell bill and its counterpart in the House went nowhere because members of Congress were unwilling to appropriate money until it was certain that Spain would sell the island.[10]

Once again Blaine entered the fray, this time not as a partisan journalist but as a newly elected Republican member of the Maine legislature. In February 1859, during debate on a series of Resolves dealing with the Buchanan-Slidell measure, Blaine urged his colleagues in the Maine House of Representatives to send a strong message to Washington opposing this speculative scheme to purchase Cuba. His objections to this Democratic, pro-slavery proposal were based primarily, but not entirely, on the anti-slavery ideology of the new Republican party. First, Blaine charged that acquiring Cuba would add several slave states to the Union and enhance the slave power's control of the federal government. Second, he feared an open-ended appropriation of this sort was a dangerous precedent that would undercut the authority of Congress and enhance executive power. Finally, betraying the racist views he shared with most of his contemporaries, Blaine charged that the "mixed and mongrel people" of the island of Cuba would be too difficult for the United States to digest and assimilate. Although the actions of the Maine legislature had little impact on the debate in the federal Congress, this expression of opposition to the Cuban purchase scheme revealed Blaine's thinking on this important foreign policy issue.[11]

The diplomatic and political machinations surrounding the 1850s efforts to annex Hawaii and Cuba may have marked Blaine's initiation into the realm of foreign relations, but during his time as editor, before becoming a state legislator, he was educated as well on a broader range of international issues. The *Journal's* news coverage and editorial assessment of Commodore Matthew Perry's expedition, which successfully opened Japan to diplomatic contact with the international community in 1854, revealed Blaine's early awareness of the growing importance of securing foreign markets for American exports and fostering the nation's overseas economic expansion. Editor Blaine also closely observed the course of the Crimean War in which Great Britain and France sought to check czarist Russia's imperial ambitions, and in true Yankee trader fashion, speculated about the possibilities for future American trade with a defeated Russia. He also took pride in the United States' recent showcasing of its agricultural and industrial progress at London's Crystal Palace Exhibition and favored American participation in upcoming international fairs, which were all the rage, as a novel way to help expand Maine's and the nation's exports.

Another dispute, in this case stemming from a budding Anglo-American imperial rivalry in the Western Hemisphere, that flared up in the 1850s and honed and sharpened Blaine's foreign policy acumen in these pre–Civil War years was the controversy surrounding the Clayton-Bulwer Treaty. Negotiated in 1850 by Secretary of State John M. Clayton and the British minister to the United States, Sir Henry L. Bulwer, this agreement attempted to adjust differences the two nations had concerning Central America and a future isthmian canal—without, of course, consulting the governments and people of that region. A classic diplomatic compromise that was deliberately ambiguous in its wording, the treaty stipulated that neither the United States nor Great Britain would have exclusive control over canal routes. Each nation also agreed to guarantee the neutrality of any future isthmian canal, and to assure this neutrality both parties also pledged not to construct military fortifications along possible canal routes. Perhaps most important from the American standpoint, both countries promised not to exercise dominion or establish control over any section of Central America.

The problem with the treaty was that it lacked precision when applied to existing British imperial enclaves in Central America. Britain assumed these areas were exempt from the terms of the agreement; the Americans did not. By the mid-1850s the Pierce administration charged that the British were deliberately and systematically violating the treaty, and the Monroe Doctrine as well, by expanding their Central American possessions. The British in turn pointed to the activities of filibusters, private adventurers who took military action in foreign countries, as a thinly disguised attempt by the American government to bring several Central American nations into the Union, in much the same pattern as Texas had been annexed. As is frequently the case in imperial rivalries of this sort, each side accused the other of dishonesty and duplicity. Anglo-American relations were further strained by British recruiting in the United States of men to serve in the Crimean War. To most Americans this was yet another demonstration of the British leadership's disdain for the United States' sovereignty.

In his third annual message on December 31, 1855, President Pierce informed Congress and the American people of the "grave" nature of the nation's difficulties with Great Britain concerning Central America and the recruitment issue. The president asserted that the Clayton-Bulwer Treaty clearly stipulated that both parties pledged that neither will ever "occupy, or fortify, or colonize, or assume or exercise any dominion over Nicaragua, Costa Rica, the Mosquito Coast, or any part of Central America." The American chief executive complained that Britain had ignored these mutually agreed-upon restrictions by continuing to colonize and extend "her absolute domain" in Central America. After a lengthy recital of the details of the dispute, Pierce expressed his hope that negotiations would bring Britain to an acceptance of the original terms of the Clayton-Bulwer Treaty. President Pierce also denounced British recruitment efforts in the United States as a violation of the nation's sovereignty and its "undeniable rights of neutrality." Again, the president stopped short of a call for war, hoping instead that a negotiated settlement of Anglo-American differences was still possible.[12]

In conformity with the practice of the time, virtually the entire script of Pierce's text was reprinted in newspapers across the land, including the *Kennebec Journal*. The American public was given the opportunity to read, and then to think and talk about, the serious issues raised by the president. The extensive coverage allotted to Pierce's annual message in Blaine's newspaper included congressional responses to the message from across the political spectrum, most notably from three individuals who had in the past or would in the future head the State Department. The American signer of the treaty just five years earlier, former Secretary of State John M. Clayton, now a senator from Delaware, confirmed to the great satisfaction of his congressional colleagues that the interpretation currently placed upon the agreement by the British government was not the one that he and Bulwer had originally negotiated. Also excerpted in the *Kennebec Journal* were the remarks of Senator Lewis Cass, an Anglophobic Democrat from Michigan who a few years hence would serve as secretary of state in James Buchanan's administration. Cass decried recent British actions in Central America as direct violations of the treaty and the basic tenets of the Monroe Doctrine.

What was especially infuriating and galling to editor Blaine and Americans in general, no matter their political persuasion, was the obvious arrogance of the British leaders and their transparent disdain for American honor and sovereignty. The recruitment issue, which personified this disdain, quickly disappeared as an irritant to wounded American pride when London recalled home the overzealous diplomat deemed responsible for this public relations fiasco. However, in the congressional debates and in countless newspaper editorials, British Prime Minister Lord Palmerston continued to be singled out as the most egregious example of British insolence and he frequently was pronounced the archenemy of the American republic. In fact, Senator Cass expressed a widespread belief among his countrymen that the "difficulty between England and the United States would never be settled while Lord Palmerston was at the head of the British ministry."[13]

Blaine assigned the most column space to Senator William H. Seward of New York, who later would be secretary of state in the administrations of Abraham Lincoln and Andrew Johnson. Seward, a prominent founder of the Republican party, and to whom Blaine turned as political role model and foreign policy mentor, warned Americans that this dispute might lead to war with Britain. But Seward sensibly counseled a waiting period with "a notice to Great Britain, that we shall interfere to prevent her exercise of dominion in South America, if it shall not be discontinued in one year." Given this time for reconsideration, the New Yorker doubted Britain would choose war because a "war will embarrass her prosperous industrial system, and could bring to her in return no adequate advantage, even if she were successful." Seward believed that the American positions were just and American demands correct; he advised his countrymen to remain firm and resolute, and "this day will inaugurate a new and important and yet a peaceful triumph over the ancient colonial policy of Europe, honorable to ourselves and auspicious to all nations."[14]

These suspicions of the English leadership's attitudes toward the

United States were well founded. Palmerston and other British leaders did hold the government and the American people in utter contempt. In his private correspondence, which now is available to scholars, Palmerston referred to Americans as "such ingenious Rogues" and said to his foreign secretary, Lord Clarendon, that "these Yankees are most disagreeable Fellows to have to do with about any American question." Clarendon wholeheartedly agreed with the prime minister, labeling the United States a "nation of Pirates," and he mocked Yankee bravado with his sneering comment to Palmerston about Britain's need to save itself from being "whipped by the greatest nation on *airth.*" To contemporary observers such as Blaine, who did not have access to the private and confidential letters of the likes of Palmerston and Clarendon, the British leadership's haughty disregard for America was all too apparent in their public actions and official pronouncements.[15]

To be fair and accurate, it should be noted that, in the 1850s, not all of the British nobility shared the anti-American outlook of Lords Palmerston and Clarendon. Lord Malmesbury, a political rival of Palmerston's who served as foreign secretary in 1858–59, expressed support privately, if not publicly, for the Americans and their Monroe Doctrine. Because of Palmerston's intransigence, President James Buchanan in December 1857 called for the abrogation of the Clayton-Bulwer Treaty. The following spring, during a meeting with George Dallas, the American minister, Lord Malmesbury, the new head of the Foreign Office, suggested arbitration of the Clayton-Bulwer dispute. Speaking more generally of Anglo-American differences, Malmesbury acknowledged that the Monroe Doctrine "was right" and believed that the British must agree to it, for "it is folly for us to oppose what everybody sees must be,—and what is natural and just—your occupancy of the whole Continent."[16]

Lord Palmerston reluctantly acceded, at least in part, to the logic of this conclusion. In 1860, once again in office as prime minister, he conceded defeat in Central America by fully accepting the American construction of the Clayton-Bulwer Treaty. However, Palmerston did not go so far as to accept Malmesbury's sweeping interpretation of the Monroe Doctrine.

President Buchanan was satisfied with Palmerston's acceptance of the American interpretation of the treaty and dropped his proposal to abrogate the Clayton-Bulwer agreement. For the time being at least, the threat of an ugly clash between the two English-speaking nations was averted, primarily because Great Britain had acquiesced to American demands. But the 1850 treaty lived on to bedevil Anglo-American relations for the remainder of the nineteenth century.

For James G. Blaine of Maine, now a promising Republican leader on the threshold of a national political career, the late 1850s pre–Civil War contretemps with Great Britain was highly instructive. To begin with, the Clayton-Bulwer controversy clarified his thinking about the ongoing Anglo-American rivalry for political and economic hegemony in the Caribbean Basin and throughout Latin America. Without question, Britain presented the main obstacle to his nation's future hemispheric ambitions. This realization inspired Blaine's nascent Anglophobia, and this resentment of Great Britain was an early source of his anti-British nationalism. Along with the majority of his fellow Americans at midcentury, Blaine distrusted the British because of their perceived record of diplomatic perfidy, only reinforced by Britain's recent actions in Central America, and resented the cavalier and dismissive treatment the British afforded the United States as a player in the international arena. Nonetheless, in 1860, Blaine probably shared Buchanan's satisfaction with the favorable resolution of the Clayton-Bulwer crisis, although some twenty years later when he became secretary of state he would be far less sanguine that the outcome served the long-range national interests of the United States.

As the result of his close and careful monitoring of the foreign policy controversies of the 1850s while editing a small but influential local newspaper, Blaine acquired a solid understanding of world events and formed decided opinions about America's future mission in the world. His earlier youthful enthusiasm for imperial expansion in the Caribbean and the Pacific may have been dampened somewhat by the competing territorial ambitions of the slave power, but at age thirty he was a fairly sophisticated and well-informed internationalist who favored an expanded global role for the United States. By no means had he prepared a finished set of blueprints for American empire at this point in his career; he had only begun to sketch out in his mind what would become the preliminary drafts for this imperial venture. But, after almost a decade of preparation, James G. Blaine was ready and eager to move on to the national stage in pursuit of personal political fortune and on behalf of his country's glorious destiny.

Notes

1. Quoted in James Wilson Pierce, *Life of James G. Blaine* (Baltimore: R. H. Woodward and Company, 1893), 23. Washington and Jefferson College does not possess a copy of this address but has a record that Blaine presented the "English salutatory" in September 1847.

2. Ibid., 26. In 1848 Blaine wrote a friend that "Kentucky has been ruined by slavery." See Blaine to Thomas B. Searight, January 14, 1848, quoted in Gail Hamilton, *Biography of James G. Blaine* (Norwich, CT: Henry Bill Publishing Company, 1895), 91.

3. Ralph S. Kuykendall, *The Hawaiian Kingdom, 1778–1854, Foundation and Transformation,* ——vols. (Honolulu: University of Hawaii Press, 1968), 1:404; Senate Executive Document No. 77, 52d Cong., 2d sess. (Washington, DC: Government Printing Office, 1893), 91–98.

4. Speech of Israel Washburn, Jr. on the Sandwich Islands, January 4, 1854, House of Representatives, *Congressional Globe,* 33d Cong., 1st sess., Appendix (Washington, DC: Office of John C. Rives, 1854), 55–59.

5. *Kennebec Journal,* November 10, 17, 24, December 1, 15, 1854.

6. Ibid., March 30, 1855.

7. Ibid., September 29, 1854.

8. James D. Richardson, *Messages and Papers of the Presidents,* 11 vols. (Washington, DC: Bureau of National Literature and Art, 1905), 5:198.

9. Kirk H. Porter and Donald Bruce Johnson, *National Party Platforms, 1840–1968* (Urbana: University of Illinois Press, 1970), 28.

10. Richardson, *Messages,* 5:511.

11. Quoted in Russell H. Conwell, *The Life and Public Service of James G. Blaine* (Hartford, CT: S. S. Scranton and Company, 1884), 125–30.

12. Richardson, *Messages,* 5:328–29.

13. Remarks of Lewis Cass, January 28, 1856, *Congressional Globe,* 34th Cong., 1st sess., Appendix (Washington, DC: 1856), 67–73.

14. *Kennebec Journal,* February 11, 1856.

15. Quoted in Kenneth Bourne, *Britain and the Balance of Power in North America, 1815–1908* (London: Longmans, Green and Company, 1967), 193–205.

16. Sarah Agnes Wallace and Frances Elma Gillespie, eds., *The Journal of Benjamin Moran, 1857–1865,* 2 vols. (Chicago: University of Chicago Press, 1948), 1:286–87.

2

Success and Fame on the National Scene

> With such amplitude and affluence of resources, and with such a vast stake at issue, we should be unworthy of our lineage and our inheritance if we for one moment distrusted our ability to maintain ourselves a united people, with 'one country, one Constitution, one destiny.'
> —James G. Blaine, 1864

In the autumn of 1860 at age thirty, James G. Blaine made his final career move. He sold his interest in the *Kennebec Journal,* vacated his editor's chair, and quit journalism to become a lifelong professional politician. To enter the public arena was a relatively easy decision for a man described by all who met him as dashing, brilliant, physically attractive and imposing, and someone obviously destined for a great future on the national scene. Besides, Blaine relished the game of politics and was good at it. He already had distinguished himself in the state legislature where, after only two years service, he was unanimously selected by his fellow lawmakers to be speaker of the lower house. In further recognition of his political talents, the young editor and aspiring public figure also had been named chair of the Maine Republican State Committee, which became his political power base for more than two decades until he resigned in 1881 to accept the position of secretary of state in James Garfield's administration.

Blaine's last hurrah as an editor came just before he left the Augusta newspaper. During the 1860 presidential campaign he devoted his news and editorial columns to the cause of the Republican candidate, Abraham Lincoln. Having been in Illinois at the time of the famous Lincoln-Douglas debates, Blaine twice observed his new hero in action. He became an immediate and enthusiastic advocate of the unpretentious railsplitter. As a convert to the Illinoisan's cause, Blaine traveled by train to the Chicago convention with Governor Lot Morrill of Maine. The two men argued throughout the journey, and by the time they reached their destination Blaine had convinced Morrill to support Lincoln. When his man won the nomination, Blaine conceded to the doubting folks back in Maine that at first glance Lincoln appeared an odd pick as the Republican party's standard-bearer. Admittedly, Lincoln was gangly and awkward, but to the skeptics Blaine countered that in "honest Abe's" case it was the "awkwardness of genius." By all accounts, editor Blaine's final partisan foray was a resounding success that helped swing Maine to the Republican column for the victorious Lincoln.

The newspaper business had been a boon to Blaine. Journalism not only launched his entry into politics, the enterprise also produced a handsome profit, which in turn allowed Blaine to become a thriving and successful entrepreneur. Early on the ambitious journalist and future public servant invested his newspaper earnings in coal properties and speculated in land purchases in his native western Pennsylvania. During and after the Civil War these proved shrewd investments that paid sizeable dividends, especially after industrialists such as Andrew Carnegie, who later became Blaine's close friend and political confidante, constructed and consolidated Pittsburgh's mammoth steel manufacturing complex. In the 1860s and 1870s James G. Blaine unquestionably was a man on the make. But, at least according to the charges leveled by his numerous critics and political adversaries, the Maine Republican's relentless chase after the almighty dollar had a predictable outcome—it undermined his moral principles and ultimately led him to violate the public trust. Right or wrong, many Americans then, and now for that matter, identified Blaine as the symbol of an era labeled the "Gilded Age" by Mark Twain because of its rampant and shameless political corruption.

As an enterprising capitalist and partisan politician, Blaine saw nothing inconsistent or shameful in combining public service with an ongoing quest for personal financial gain. Throughout his time on the national stage he persistently denied any wrongdoing. Besides, he enjoyed creature comforts and the material trappings of financial success, which to his mind were the justified rewards and perks of the system. A devoted family man, Blaine took pride in being able to purchase for $5,000 cash a large, stately mansion in Augusta as a birthday gift for his wife in 1862, to have a number of household servants and a full-time personal secretary, and to send his children abroad for their education. He easily could afford to travel to Europe, as he did in 1867 and again with his family in the late 1880s to visit the Carnegies in Scotland, hobnob with European aristocracy, and tour the Continent. Blaine also had the financial means to build a fine home on Dupont Circle in the nation's capital and a spacious seaside summer "cottage" at Bar Harbor in Maine. In Gilded Age America such ostentatious spending was a hallmark of success, an unmistakable sign that one, along with the Vanderbilts, the Rockefellers, and the Carnegies, indeed had made it big.

Another characteristic of this "age of excess" was an abiding faith in the benefits and virtues of progress. Blaine was a true believer in this "culture of progress," which emphasized, among other things, economic growth, technological advancement, and market expansion at home and abroad. For nineteenth-century Americans progress was tied not only to individual gain and improvement, but to the nation's destiny and future glory as well. Consequently, when the slave states seceded and created the Confederacy in 1861, Blaine, along with most of his fellow Republicans, enthusiastically supported Abraham Lincoln's vigorous prosecution of the war against the rebellious South. In this instance, progress meant purifying the republic by cleansing the nation of the scourge of slavery and ending once and for all the threat posed by the continued expansion of the slave power. Even as the Civil War tore the nation apart, Blaine retained his faith in the future greatness and destiny of the United States. Only in this context could the war's indescribable horror and terrible bloodshed have meaning and purpose.

Immediately upon the outbreak of hostilities, Blaine used his position in the Maine legislature to supply troops and military aid to the Union cause. To coordinate his state's banner effort in repeatedly meeting its quota of men and material in the early years of the war, he served as liaison between Maine Governor Israel Washburn, Jr., and the new vice president, Hannibal Hamlin, both of whom were Maine Republicans, and Blaine's own veteran political allies. Although intensely loyal to the Union, citizen Blaine chose not to join the army. Instead he hired a substitute to serve in his place, a fairly common practice in the North during the Civil War. But for an ambitious politician with aspirations for national office, it was unusual and a little risky to pass up the future opportunity to appeal to the electorate as a military hero on horseback. Every Republican candidate for the presidency from General Ulysses S. Grant in 1868 to Major William McKinley in 1896, save Blaine in 1884, had been an officer in the Union army. While Blaine's patriotism was not challenged during the war years, questions about his failure to volunteer for the army were raised in the presidential campaign. The issue was ineffective, however, because Grover Cleveland, the Democratic candidate in 1884, also had chosen the substitute option and had remained a civilian during the war between the states.

James G. Blaine formally arrived on the national scene in December 1863 when he entered the House of Representatives. He had been nominated and elected the previous year as the Republican candidate for Maine's Kennebec district, but because of the odd congressional system then in practice, he had to wait more than a year before taking his seat as a member of the 38th Congress. In that fourteen-month interval not only had President Lincoln issued the Emancipation Proclamation but also the tide of battle had turned as Union armies defeated General Robert E. Lee's forces at Gettysburg in July 1863. In that same month General Grant captured Vicksburg, opening the Mississippi River to unimpeded navigation and splitting the Confederacy in two. Although Union victory now seemed assured, President Lincoln, in his address delivered at the dedication of the cemetery at Gettysburg only a few weeks before Blaine came to Washington, reminded Americans what was at stake: "that we here highly resolve that these dead shall not have died in vain—that this nation, under God, shall have a new birth of freedom—and that government of the people, by the people, for the people, shall not perish from the earth."[1]

Blaine had campaigned for the House seat on the sole promise that he would "stand heartily and unreservedly" behind the administration because "the fate of the American Union" was dependent on the success of Abraham Lincoln. Over the course of the remainder of the war, the freshman congressman kept his promise to Maine voters, never faltering in his allegiance to Lincoln. He fervently shared his political idol's faith in the prospect of "a new birth of freedom" for all Americans. In his first major speech on the floor of the House in April 1864, dealing with the federal government's ability to assume the war debts of the loyal states, Blaine publicly proclaimed his hopes and dreams for the glorious destiny that awaited a victorious United States. Framing his vision for national glory almost exclusively in the context of "the great elements of material progress," Blaine believed that Americans were assured "the grandest future reserved for any people" because the nation's virtually unlimited resources and expansive territory guaranteed "the acquisition and consolidation of wealth, varied, magnificent, and immeasurable." All that was needed to reap the rewards of national greatness, according to Congressman Blaine, was for supporters of the Union to stay the course to final victory; thereafter, the United States would emerge once again as a united people with "one country, one Constitution, one destiny."[2]

On closer scrutiny it was apparent that in his initial congressional speech Blaine blended two of the most prominent themes of antebellum expansionist ideology. The first of these was the widely held belief, which had originated in James Madison's *Federalist #10* with the concept of "extending the sphere," that unending territorial expansion was the epoxy of the Union because it would allay and overcome sectionalism. For example, this pervasive faith in the unifying power of territorial growth led Israel Washburn, Jr., who had helped Blaine organize the Republican party in Maine, to maintain during the sectional crisis of the 1850s that continental and overseas expansion would "bind us more indissolubly together. We cannot fly apart." Lincoln explicitly had said "no" to this antebellum axiom when it meant slavery's continued expansion, and the ensuing Civil War brutally challenged the veracity of this expansionist dogma. Yet here was Blaine amidst a devastating war brought on by sectional strife arguing the old line about how settling and peopling the nation's western domain and creating many more states would "add to the strength and insure the perpetuity of our Government." The Maine Republican predicted, incorrectly as it turned out, that forty new states would be carved from the western territories for "a grand total of seventy-five prosperous Commonwealths" by the year 1900.[3]

Blaine undoubtedly agreed with Lincoln on the need for a rebirth of freedom, but he clearly did not accept his political mentor's outright rejection of the "extend the sphere" panacea. In this case, Blaine's vision reached beyond that of Lincoln's, whose sole great mission was to save the Union. As a self-appointed spokesman for the next generation of Republican leaders, Blaine looked beyond the Civil War and understood that territorial consolidation, now happily freed of the slave power's threatening grip, was essential to the fulfillment of the second antebellum expansionist axiom touched upon in his speech. This second axiom held that overseas territorial and economic expansion were the key ingredients for the creation of a formal American empire on the pattern of the nineteenth-century British empire. However, even before the outbreak of the Civil War, this axiom was being modified by some of its adherents who stressed that commercial expansion and the establishment of an informal empire were preferable to colonialism on the European model.

At this stage of the intellectual and ideological maturation of his foreign policy agenda, James G. Blaine was an informal empire man. In 1864 his updated imperial blueprints were grounded on the assumption that the United States would soon establish global economic hegemony. To accomplish international marketplace predominance, which was the backbone of informal empire, a nation needed bound-less economic growth and material progress based upon unrivaled agricultural and manufacturing production. Blaine believed these pre-requisites for informal empire were being met, particularly in agricul-ture, "giving us so far the lead in the production of those staple articles essential to life and civilization that we become the arbiter of the world's destiny without aiming at the world's empire." If a reunited American republic never quite achieved that international status dur-ing Blaine's lifetime, his optimistic forecast for national greatness was nonetheless prophetic: by the midtwentieth century the United States unquestionably had assumed the role of world arbiter and become a global superpower.[4]

Throughout the remainder of the war and in the immediate post-war years, Blaine continued to reformulate and redraft his blueprints for American empire. Prior to his speech on the debt issue, he had voted in favor of a joint House resolution sponsored by Republican Henry Winter Davis of Maryland, deploring French intervention in Mexico and declaring "it does not accord with the policy of the United States to acknowledge any monarchical Government erected on the ruins of any republican Government in America." Davis's resolution implicitly challenged Secretary of State William H. Seward to use the Monroe Doctrine to uphold American interests in the Western Hemi-sphere. In the spring of 1864 many members of Congress, especially House Republicans, were puzzled as to why the Lincoln administra-tion had failed to invoke the doctrine in response to France's over-throw of the government of Benito Juárez and its installation of the Archduke Maximilian of Austria as emperor of Mexico. A nervous and cautious Seward had neither employed the Monroe Doctrine nor lodged a formal protest with France because he feared it would throw the French into the arms of the South and lead to their formal recog-nition of the Confederacy. Seward's expedient diplomacy aided the Union cause by forestalling French recognition of the Confederacy, but the Mexicans must be credited with upholding the Monroe Doctrine. In 1867 Juárez's forces, without the aid of their North American neigh-bor, ousted the French, restored Mexican rule, and executed by firing squad the "Arch-Dupe," as some antimonarchical Americans deri-sively labeled the hapless Maximilian.[5]

The congressional and public debate over France's meddling in Mexico strongly influenced James G. Blaine's thinking about the United States' proper future role in Latin America. His Pan-Americanism origi-nally may have been inspired by his admiration for Henry Clay's ear-lier vision of hemispheric cooperation. But the 1860s discussion of the

validity and usefulness of Monroe's 1823 declaration as a means to prevent European political and military intervention in the New World
also was a seminal source of Blaine's future Latin American policy.
Blaine took to heart and was guided by his colleague Henry Winter
Davis's advice for the direction of the Republican party's long-range
policy in the Western Hemisphere. In defending his resolution on the
floor of the House, Davis had provided a clear statement of the Republican goals in Latin America: "We wish to cultivate friendship with our
republican brethren of Mexico and South America, to aid in consoli-
dating republican principles, to retain popular government in all this
continent from the fangs of monarchical or aristocratic power, and to
lead the sisterhood of American republics in the paths of peace, prosperity, and power." It no longer should be a mystery as to where Blaine
"found" his policy of Pan-Americanism. Years later, as secretary of
state, the Maine Republican would follow Davis's agenda almost to the
letter.[6]

During the summer and fall of 1864, Blaine backed President Lincoln's successful campaign for a second term; heartily endorsed the
party platform, especially the plank objecting to European interference in Latin America; and once again helped secure Maine's electoral
vote for the Republican ticket. After the election, when the 38th Congress convened in December for its second session, Blaine demonstrated anew his loyalty to the Lincoln administration. Henry Winter
Davis was impatient with Seward's careful diplomacy and frustrated
that his resolution opposing French intervention in Mexico had failed
to goad the State Department into action. To get the executive branch
moving, Representative Davis offered another resolution on December 15, 1864, asserting that Congress had the constitutional right "to
an authoritative voice in declaring and prescribing the foreign policy
of the United States" and that it was the duty of the president to respect such policy, which in this case meant acting to force France out
of Mexico.[7]

On this occasion Blaine parted company with his fellow Republican and sometime congressional mentor. Explaining that he objected
to "even an implied censure" of the president and secretary of state
and praising Seward's judicious correspondence with France on the
Mexican issue, Blaine voted with the majority of House members who
narrowly succeeded in tabling Davis's attempt to assert congressional
authority over the operation of the nation's diplomacy. It should be
recalled that only five years earlier, as a member of the Maine legislature, Blaine had opposed the Cuban policy of Democratic President
James Buchanan on constitutional grounds similar to those Davis had

adopted, arguing that the chief executive was undermining Congress's role in making foreign policy. The Maine congressman now shifted his position, partly out of partisan loyalty to Abraham Lincoln, but primarily because he had come to accept on ideological grounds the executive branch's prerogative in foreign affairs and the president's right to conduct the nation's day-to-day diplomacy. Ever after, unlike most other nineteenth-century politicians who rose to national prominence in the House of Representatives or the Senate, Blaine favored a purely oversight role for Congress and did not champion legislative control in the formulation of foreign policy. He never again veered from a basic belief in the legitimacy of executive power in the realm of foreign relations.

While the Civil War experience prompted an understandable change in Blaine's thinking about the desirability of a strong executive, it underscored as well the necessity of an energetic national government to the success of his blueprints for informal empire and global economic supremacy. Federal power, however, had to be used wisely and not vindictively. Protective tariffs were beneficial, but an export tax on cotton to punish the South was foolhardy because it would delay the restoration of an American "monopoly of this article in the markets of the world." Consequently, after the Union victory Blaine became a major Republican spokesman for overseas market expansion for commodity exports, such as cotton and wheat, and favored federal subsidies for a transcontinental railroad, overseas mail service, and the rebuilding of an American merchant marine. Also, in the immediate postwar years, tariff protection for American industry was crucial because, as Blaine explained on the floor of the House, protectionism and not free trade would guarantee that the United States "will in no long period surpass the gigantic industrial system of Great Britain."[8]

Just as U.S. hegemony in the Western Hemisphere was a bedrock in the foundation of Blaine's imperial vision, so too was his corollary belief, strongly reinforced by the British government's actions during the Civil War, that Great Britain presented the main obstacle to his nation's hemispheric and global ambitions. His Anglophobia, already apparent in his thinking during his days as a partisan journalist, became a basic tenet in Blaine's global outlook during and after the sectional conflict and guided his strategy for the fulfillment of America's destiny. The outbreak of the Civil War had been a jarring setback to Blaine's imperial dreams because the conflict threatened the existence of the Union and the United States' future position as a world power. Both the North and the South deemed Britain's stance on the war as crucial to the outcome. Jefferson Davis's government openly courted

British recognition of the Confederacy in the hope that British financial assistance and possible military intervention might guarantee the success of Southern independence. Among Republican leaders such as Blaine the belief was fairly widespread that Great Britain intended to take advantage of the conflict to strengthen its global commercial supremacy by destroying a burgeoning economic rival. Not only was such a policy wholly consistent with Blaine's perception of Britain's historic record but British actions during the war did little to dispel that view.

To begin with, Blaine resented both the London government's quick recognition of Southern belligerency in May 1861 and the early sympathy for the Confederacy expressed by a number of British politicians, including the anti-American Lord Palmerston and the great Liberal leader, William E. Gladstone. More infuriating were the efforts of a group of Conservative leaders—including Sir Robert Cecil, the marquis of Salisbury, and J. A. Roebuck—who organized the private Southern Independence Association primarily to raise funds for the Confederacy. Lord Salisbury, later prime minister when Blaine headed the State Department, doubted Great Britain and the North could ever be friends because "we aspire to the same position—rule of the seas and worldwide commercial supremacy." Roebuck made it abundantly clear why he hoped the South would succeed and not rejoin the Union: "America while she was united ran a race of prosperity unparalleled in the world. Eighty years made the Republic such a power, that if she had continued as she was a few years longer she would have been the great bully of the world."[9]

Although the British government did not heed the exhortations of Roebuck and his allies and never granted diplomatic recognition to the Confederacy, its actions and overall policy during the Civil War left a legacy of ill will that the likes of James G. Blaine never forgave or forgot. Decades after the war it still rankled him. In his best-selling two-volume book, *Twenty Years of Congress*, published in the mid-1880s, he recounted: "The civil war closed with ill-feeling amounting to resentment towards England on the part of the loyal citizens of the United States. They believed the Government of Great Britain, and especially the aristocratic and wealthy classes (whose influence in the kingdom is predominant), had desired the destruction of the Union." He also made the familiar charge that Britain's unfriendly actions, especially in allowing Confederate commerce raiders such as the *Alabama* to be built in its ports, had prolonged the war. For Blaine and many Americans, fear was no longer the primary emotional ingredient of their anti-British sentiment, as it had been in the 1840s and 1850s when the nation anxiously anticipated that Britain would stymie American territorial expansion. Instead, British actions during the Civil War embittered citizens in both the North and South and intensified throughout the country an already blossoming anti-British nationalism.[10]

In May 1867, barely two years after the Union victory, Congressman Blaine, in the tradition of his forebears, embarked on a three-month grand tour of Europe. He and his friend, fellow legislator Justin Morrill, a Republican member of Congress from Vermont, visited the British Isles, France, Germany, Belgium, Italy, and Switzerland. Their initial stop was Ireland, where Blaine, whose ancestors were from the Emerald Isle, noted "the fearful effects of *absenteeism,* and the general disaster to the native race caused by English policy." In England the traveling Americans "fell in with many English gentlemen," observed the debates in the House of Commons, and on an excursion to the Midlands were impressed with the magnitude of the Birmingham manufacturing complex. Both men were flattered by the attention they received in Parliament, where they met a number of prominent British leaders, including John Stuart Mill. A delighted Blaine ascribed all this fuss over their visit to the recent success of Northern arms: "Our war has infused a tremendous respect for us into the minds of Englishmen." This worldly and cosmopolitan son of Maine may have resented the British government's actions during the late war, but he had no personal animosity for individual Britons, nor did he allow national resentments to carry over into his personal contacts with English gentlemen and aristocrats.[11]

Upon his return to the United States, Blaine reentered the post–Civil War partisan political fray that pitted the legislative against the executive branch of federal government. He sided with his fellow congressional Republicans in their struggle with President Andrew Johnson over Reconstruction policy for the South and voted, as did every other House Republican, for the president's impeachment in February 1868. The Republicans, to ensure victory in the 1864 campaign, had temporarily recast themselves as the Union party and placed Johnson, a pro-Union Tennessee Democrat, on the ticket as their vice presidential candidate. As with many such acts of political expediency, this Faustian electoral bargain backfired on the Republicans when Lincoln was assassinated. In the White House Andrew Johnson proved much too pro-Southern for their tastes, and his presidential formula for reconstruction of the Union was anathema to the Republican leadership in Congress.

The partisan heat accompanying this executive-legislative battle also tarnished the image of Blaine's earlier political idol, William H.

Seward, a once true-blue Republican. Seward chose to remain in Johnson's cabinet after Lincoln's death and emerged as a chief defender of the administration's policies for quick readmission of the rebellious states. Clearly upset with Seward's actions, Blaine, early on in the struggle, confided to Israel Washburn, Jr.: "We are in a *Muss* here— and I suppose the rupture between Congress and the Executive will be permanent—I deeply regret it—and yet I do not see how it could have been avoided. . . . Your old friend Seward is at the bottom of the mischief." Although in later years Blaine graciously conceded "the apparent magnanimity and broad charity of Mr. Seward's line of procedure," at the time he was troubled by Seward's actions and politically distanced himself from his former mentor.[12]

Blaine's mixed feelings about Seward's lenient approach to the former Confederate states explained his lack of enthusiasm for the secretary of state's expansionist Caribbean policies, which the Maine Republican feared also might too readily reestablish a Southern ascendancy in the Union. At the end of the Civil War William H. Seward was impatient to fulfill his vision of American empire. He sought a naval base in the Dominican Republic, attempted to purchase the Danish West Indies, and toyed with the possibility of annexing Cuba. Throughout the war Secretary Seward had been constrained by diplomatic necessity to keep his imperial ambitions on the back burner, although he had occasional dealings with William and Jane Cazneau, a notorious couple who in the 1850s had close ties with the Pierce and Buchanan administrations and had been pro-slavery lobbyists for commercial expansion in the Caribbean. At a meeting with the secretary of state a few months after the Confederate surrender at Appomattox, Mrs. Cazneau initially interested Seward in the possibility of an American naval station in the Dominican Republic. In January 1866 Secretary Seward embarked on what was billed as a pleasure tour of the Caribbean, but when he visited Santo Domingo, sightseeing was not at the top of his agenda. While there Seward personally explored the feasibility of a U.S. naval facility and conferred with the president of the Dominican Republic at a meeting also attended by the Cazneaus. Later that month President Johnson, at Seward's behest, nominated William Cazneau as the United States' commissioner and consul general to the Dominican Republic.[13]

For Blaine and many other Republicans, Seward's Caribbean schemes were tainted by his collaboration with the Cazneaus. Memories of President Buchanan's expansionist actions in the Caribbean on behalf of the slave power just six or seven years earlier, aided and abetted by the lobbying of this opportunistic pro-Southern husband-wife team, were still too fresh in Blaine's mind to be forgotten or forgiven. In the debate in the House, he made no effort to support the Johnson administration's attempt to annex the Dominican Republic in 1867–68. Congressmen Blaine's coolness to this imperial venture undoubtedly stemmed from his distaste for Seward's willingness to conduct business as usual with former pro-slavery lobbyists and alleged Confederate sympathizers. Not surprisingly, Republicans in the Senate felt the same way and rejected William Cazneau's nomination as commissioner to the Dominican Republic on the suspicion that he had been a Confederate sympathizer. There were limits to Blaine's expansionist dreams: he and a number of other Republicans drew the line at associating with the likes of the Cazneaus. Empire at that price was unacceptable.

Initially, there also was some ambiguity in the Maine Republican's response to the treaty William H. Seward negotiated with Russia in 1867 to purchase Alaska. At no point in the House debate on the Alaska treaty did Blaine speak in its favor and, because he already was on the stump in Maine for General Grant's presidential campaign, was recorded as "not voting" when the appropriation bill that funded the acquisition of "Seward's icebox" was approved. Almost two decades later, after some reflection on the significance of Seward's accomplishment, Blaine, then the elder statesman of the Republican party, identified the purchase of Alaska as the national event that formally terminated the slave power's grip on continental expansion. Throughout the history of the republic, he argued in his popular book *Twenty Years of Congress*, territorial additions to the United States had been guided by the Democratic party and had "all been in the interest of slavery." He contended that looking "northward for territory, instead of southward, was a radical change of policy," one that "happily and appropriately, it was the good fortune of Mr. Seward to initiate under impressive and significant circumstances." In this highly partisan tribute to Seward, historian Blaine's selective analysis conveniently ignored the Oregon settlement and the acquisition of California, each the accomplishment of a Democratic president and both successfully opening windows on the Pacific for the commercial activities of northern merchants and entrepreneurs.[14]

Representative Blaine's transition from Seward's defender during the Lincoln years to skeptic and critic in the Johnson administration was revealed yet again in his objection to the secretary's inclusion of what amounted to an unmonitored slush fund in the State Department's budget request. In February 1868 Blaine opposed what was called the "secret-service fund," a budget line in the diplomatic appropriations bill from which the secretary of state could make expenditures without accountability or audit. Such a secret contingent fund had been a feature of the executive budget since George Washington's first administration. It was a tacit and expedient recognition by Congress of the validity of Thomas Jefferson's dictum that "the transaction of business with foreign nations is executive altogether." However, watchdog Blaine, untutored at this point in all of the nuances of executive-legislative power sharing and consistent with his belief in Congress's oversight capacity in the conduct of foreign policy, said, "I think we ought not to have in this Government any such thing as a secret-service fund." He objected to the rationale offered by its defenders: "If money be needed for Americans who get into trouble abroad let the appropriation be so limited." Despite these objections, the realities of power prevailed. The bill passed intact, and his reluctant endorsement of the secret-service fund was but one more step in the imperial education of James G. Blaine.[15]

To correct the misguided policies of President Andrew Johnson and end the apostasy of Secretary of State William H. Seward, Blaine enthusiastically endorsed the 1868 candidacy of Ulysses S. Grant, the slayer of the Confederate dragon and Union victor at Appomattox. Andrew Johnson, labeled by many Republicans as nothing more than a pro-Southern renegade Tennessee Democrat, especially disappointed Blaine because he squandered the promised fruits of Union victory. "Now Grant," he early on confided to Israel Washburn, Jr., "looms up as the savior alike of country and party—a *necessity to both*." All party loyalists confidently expected that General Grant's election would bring to the White House a true Republican leader and worthy successor to Lincoln. Barely a month after Grant's victory at the polls, Blaine, now a rising power in the Republican party on the verge of being elected speaker of the House, unveiled to the nation his guidelines for the GOP's future political and diplomatic agenda. Blaine was supremely confident, almost cocky, that under the leadership of President-elect Grant the Republicans finally would turn things around and reap the deserved rewards of the triumph of Union arms.[16]

Pursuing the partisan post–Civil War tactic known as "waving the bloody shirt," which he would resort to repeatedly over the next decade, Blaine cast the Democrats as the perpetrators of rebellion and identified the Republican party and the Union as synonymous. But his performance was notable for more than the standard bloody shirt routine. Personally committed to the ideal of racial justice, Blaine in an

1868 address on the House floor spoke directly to the issue of racial violence and the mounting tensions between Southern whites and recently freed blacks. He was hopeful that racial intolerance could be overcome and optimistically projected ahead to the 1876 centennial of the nation's birth as a time when "the patriotic conduct of the one class and the softening of unreasonable prejudice toward the other, will enable the American people to hold the centennial celebration of their independence with no citizen of the Republic disfranchised, and with the sublime declaration that 'all men are created equal' accepted and realized on the hundredth anniversary of its majestic utterance." Once again, Blaine demonstrated that his vision extended beyond that of his idol, the Great Emancipator. The Maine Republican courageously championed black equality, an ideal for American democracy that Lincoln throughout his life had doubted was attainable.[17]

Blaine was equally optimistic about the future of the nation's diplomacy. The incoming Grant administration would place the United States on a true path to its national destiny by establishing "a higher standard of American citizenship—with more dignity and character to the name abroad and more assured liberty and security attaching to it at home." Bitterly remembering the embarrassment of the antebellum years when the republic's foreign relations were being dictated by the slave power, Blaine prophesied a new era of national greatness in which American "diplomacy will be rescued from the subservient tone by which we have so often been humiliated in our own eyes and in the eyes of Europe, and the true position of the first nation of the earth in rank and prestige will be asserted; not in spirit of bravado or with the mere arrogance of strength, but with the conscious dignity which belongs to power, and with the moderation which is the true ornament of justice." His blueprints for empire clearly had passed through another stage of revision and refinement.[18]

Several questions arise from Blaine's unequivocal endorsement of this man on horseback. Why on earth did James G. Blaine have such high expectations of Ulysses S. Grant? Why did he have such great faith in an untested political leader who never previously had been elected to public office, who initially abandoned a military career and had been a failure in civilian life before his Civil War battlefield exploits catapulted him to national prominence? Unquestionably, Blaine backed the Union general because he believed his popularity among the American public would assure Republican victory in 1868. But, arguably, Blaine supported Grant primarily because he believed the general to be a kindred spirit in the quest for empire and the pursuit of national greatness. Grant was a fellow Anglophobe who distrusted and feared Britain. He and Blaine were tutored in the late 1860s by Henry C. Carey, the pioneer economist. Through occasional attendance at Carey's weekly "Vespers," Grant and Blaine learned the ABCs of tariff protectionism and economic nationalism. As part of his comprehensive program for the realization of the United States' commercial, financial, and industrial independence, Carey offered his pupils lessons on anti-British nationalism and "how to outdo England without fighting her." Grant and Blaine shared as well the Republican party's commitment to an activist and energetic national government that would promote overseas commercial expansion and the construction of an interoceanic canal.[19]

Ulysses S. Grant's awareness of the need for an isthmian canal in Central America was long-standing and etched in his memory by a bitter experience as a young army officer. In July 1852 then Captain Grant led a military party of several hundred soldiers and their families, bound for garrison duty in the new state of California, in a harrowing trek across Panama that left 150 dead, including men, women, and children. When he entered the White House in 1869, President Grant was determined to find a way to build an interoceanic canal, which would end the necessity for embarking on such grueling passages across the isthmus. He thought the project was feasible from an engineering and technological standpoint, but feared Europeans might construct a canal before the United States did, especially in light of the recent French success at Suez. "I regard it as of vast political importance to this country that no European government should hold such a work," Grant proclaimed, and commended to the American people "an American canal, on American soil." To forestall a possible European isthmian canal enterprise, Grant, during his two presidential terms, sponsored seven technical expeditions to Central America to determine the proper location for a man-made water corridor. All to no avail, because in the 1870s public opinion and congressional support lagged behind Grant's executive initiatives.[20]

Undoubtedly, President Grant's first annual message further assured Speaker Blaine that the two of them were on the same wavelength as well when it came to global trade competition and the search for foreign markets. The completion and extension of railroads on the European continent and in Asia, Grant observed, were "bringing into competition with our agricultural products like products of other countries." This new competitive challenge "teaches us also the necessity of looking to other markets for the sale of our surplus. Our neighbors south of us, and China and Japan, should receive our special attention. It will be the endeavor of the Administration to cultivate such relations with all these nations as to entitle us to their confidence and make it their interest, as well as ours, to establish better commercial relations." Among members of the executive branch during Grant's presidency the commitment to market expansion ran deep. For example, one Treasury Department official claimed America's future security and prosperity called for the "extension of the Monroe Doctrine to the commerce of the continent."[21]

In an attempt to ensure that the Grant administration's diplomacy would be energetic and assertive, James G. Blaine sought to influence the appointment of the new secretary of state. Just after the 1868 presidential election the would-be kingmaker once again used the powerful Maine Republican network. He wrote his old friend Elihu Washburne, who also was a former editor of the *Kennebec Journal*, urging the Illinois congressman to use his political clout with the newly elected president to secure the appointment of an aggressive, patriotic individual to head the State Department. Perhaps Blaine had himself in mind when he recommended to Washburne that the appointee be someone favorable to overseas economic expansion who would stand up to Great Britain and vigorously pursue the course of national destiny and national greatness. Blaine's advice fell on deaf ears. In one of the more bizarre incidents in American diplomatic history, Grant appointed Elihu Washburne as secretary of state, a post he occupied for just twelve days—March 5–16, 1869—the shortest time on record for any holder of that office. Apparently a courtesy appointment, bestowed by a grateful Grant to honor his patron and crony from Galena, Washburne immediately upon his resignation from State was approved as minister to France and remained as American envoy in Paris until 1877, serving with distinction during the 1871 upheaval of the Commune. Hamilton Fish of New York, a conservative Republican with experience in both the House and Senate and an acceptable choice to Blaine, was Washburne's successor as secretary of state. Fish held the office until the end of Grant's second term.[22]

Undeterred by his failure to influence Grant's selection of a new secretary of state, Blaine persistently sought diplomatic appointments for at least two of his friends who were loyal Republicans—a common practice then as now. After becoming speaker of the House in March 1869, he pushed to have John L. Stevens, his coeditor during his newspaper days in Augusta and fellow advocate of Hawaiian annexation in the mid-1850s, appointed as commissioner to the Sandwich Islands. Stevens did not receive the Hawaiian posting, but instead was named minister to Uruguay and Paraguay, where he served from 1870 to 1873. In that heady spring of 1869 a confident Blaine also sought to have a friend selected as U.S. consul at Foochow, China, but without success. Despite his solid support in behalf of Grant's election, the new speaker discovered his power to influence diplomatic appointments was limited. However, at one point President Grant did contemplate sending Blaine to London as American minister to Great Britain, but in the end rejected the idea. Blaine probably did not know he was being considered for this prestigious diplomatic appointment and probably never was a serious candidate for the London mission. He was more useful to the administration as House speaker, where he shone as a master parliamentary tactician and party loyalist.[23]

Overall, the Grant administration's handling of Anglo-American relations pleased Blaine and substantially, if not completely, fulfilled his earlier expectations about the arrival of a new era in American diplomacy. Secretary of State Fish proved resilient, even at times tenacious, in his negotiations with the British over several contentious issues stemming from the Civil War years. Some old scores were settled; the nation's honor and prestige were being upheld. This was especially true of the 1871 Treaty of Washington in which Great Britain expressed regret "for the escape, under whatever circumstances, of the *Alabama* and other vessels from British ports, and for the depredations committed by those vessels." Along with this expression of regret, the Anglo-American agreement provided for international arbitration of the *Alabama* claims by a five-member tribunal. Sweeter still for Anglophobes like Blaine, the Treaty of Washington verified the American principle of acquired nationality. Although the time had long since passed when the Royal Navy's officers could impress American seamen and debase American citizenship on the high seas with the haughty cry "once an Englishman, always an Englishman," the British government's formal recognition of the legitimacy of naturalized citizenship did happily, if belatedly, vindicate American national honor.[24]

When the five-member tribunal met later that year in Geneva, Switzerland, to arbitrate the *Alabama* claims, the United States stunned and infuriated the British by reviving the issue of "indirect damages." An outlandish bit of jingoism that was framed with the upcoming 1872 presidential election campaign in mind, the indirect damage claim called for Great Britain to pay all the costs of the Civil War "after the battle of Gettysburg" with 7 percent interest. Was it any wonder that British leaders were angry? They assumed these ridiculous nuisance claims had been dispensed with by mutual agreement earlier on in the treaty negotiations. However, Blaine applauded this public goading of the British lion and when Fish's resolve appeared to weaken in the following months, the speaker was at the secretary's doorstep to stiffen his spine. On several occasions during the spring of 1872, either on his own initiative or by invitation, the speaker was included with Fish and other members of Grant's cabinet in private discussions on the status of Anglo-American relations. In a letter of May 1, 1872, to her son Walker, Harriet Blaine reported, "Everything political, English and American, seems to be in sort of a snarl." "Your Father," she continued, went to Secretary Fish's home "to talk over matters with him Sunday evening. Was there till a very late hour. Commercial interests bring heavily to bear on the question." Shortly after this meeting Blaine followed up with a personal letter to Fish stressing that it "is of immense consequence to our national prestige that we now stand firm."[25]

Blaine relished being a foreign policy insider and was pleased to be included as a regular participant in the Grant administration's deliberations on the course of Anglo-American relations. Although the international tribunal wisely rejected the indirect damages argument—to the relief, as it turned out, of both American and British statesmen—the overall settlement of the *Alabama* claims was highly favorable to the United States. In September 1872, at the height of Grant's reelection campaign, the five-member tribunal announced an indemnity award of $15.5 million. The British arbitrator on the panel, Sir Alexander Cockburn, was aghast that his country would have to pay such a large monetary indemnity. He refused to sign and registered his dissent. But in the end the British government paid up. Not incidentally, President Grant was easily reelected to a second term in November. Speaker Blaine was elated with the *Alabama* settlement and the GOP victory at the polls. He publicly praised his fellow Republicans for their success in resolving Anglo-American disputes without sacrificing national honor. In his book, *Twenty Years of Congress*, historian Blaine decreed that President Grant and Secretary Fish were "entitled to the highest credit" for their diplomatic triumph.[26]

Not all aspects of Grant's diplomacy received Speaker Blaine's support and approval, however. He had serious disagreements with the administration over its Caribbean policy. From the time he arrived in the White House, President Grant had been keen on the annexation of the Dominican Republic because it would enhance American trade and commerce in the Caribbean. Grant's desire to annex the island republic also was fueled by his ambitions for an isthmian canal. The president believed that an American naval base at Samana Bay would safeguard the Caribbean entrance to the proposed interoceanic waterway. Blaine was unpersuaded by Grant's arguments. Only a few years earlier he had opposed Secretary of State Seward's schemes for Caribbean territorial expansion and in the interim had not changed his mind about the undesirability of Caribbean annexations. True, in 1869 a number of his Republican House colleagues such as John A. Logan, Ben Butler, and Nathaniel Banks were on the annexation bandwagon, but Blaine was not swayed because the cast of characters pushing the Dominican treaty still included the unsavory and objectionable husband-wife duo, William and Jane Cazneau. Their expansionist activities in the 1850s and early 1860s in behalf of the slave South and the Confederacy still rankled Congressman Blaine; he consistently rejected any Caribbean annexationist effort in which the Cazneaus played a leading role.

President Grant worked hard to change the speaker's mind, but no amount of personal arm-twisting overcame Blaine's opposition to Dominican annexation. After one of these arm-twisting sessions in early January 1871, Blaine confided to a friend: "I have been round to the White House since dinner to call on the President. He sent for me, and we had a frank chat on Santo Domingo. I will support the resolution of inquiry, but am against the final acquisition." In his enthusiasm for Caribbean expansion, Grant also lobbied hard to gain the support of Senator Charles Sumner of Massachusetts. As chair of the Senate Foreign Relations Committee, Sumner's backing for the annexation treaty was crucial to its success. After a discussion of the Dominican issue at the Senator's home one evening, Grant believed he had obtained Sumner's agreement to be one of the main backers of the treaty in the Senate. When Senator Sumner came out in strong opposition to the annexation treaty a short time later, Grant felt he had been betrayed and reacted angrily to what he believed was Sumner's duplicity. A bitter intraparty feud ensued. Grant maneuvered to have Sumner purged as chair of the Foreign Relations Committee, but even that drastic action failed to secure enough votes and, consequently, the Senate never ratified the Dominican treaty. Speaker Blaine, who wisely distanced himself from this Republican party bloodletting, probably shared Senator Sumner's dismay that President Grant, in his schemes for Caribbean empire, was following the example of his pro-Southern predecessors, Franklin Pierce, James Buchanan, and Andrew Johnson.[27]

Despite his serious disagreement with Grant over Caribbean expansion, Blaine was more than satisfied with the administration's overall handling of the nation's foreign relations. The president and speaker remained on friendly, even warm, terms throughout the rancorous political struggle over Dominican annexation. In the autumn of 1871, President and Mrs. Grant visited the Blaines in Maine and throughout the next year's reelection campaign Speaker Blaine was on the hustings, at one stage even venturing South with the noted black abolitionist, Frederick Douglass, to seek votes for the GOP ticket in Virginia and North Carolina. With Grant safely ensconced in the White House for another four years, the future of the republic seemed secure. For the remainder of his tenure as speaker of the House until 1875, when the Democrats gained control of the House for the first time since the Civil War, Blaine took great pride in his nation's burgeoning international prestige and global stature. He relished international recognition of America's economic and political triumphs and enjoyed officially greeting foreign delegations who sought help and guidance from the model republic, including the Iwakura mission from Japan and the visit of the Hawaiian king, Kalakaua, and his entourage. Japan and Hawaii definitely were on his imperial map and integral to his blueprints for future American dominance in the Pacific Rim.

In December 1871 Lord Iwakura Tomomi and his party of more than one hundred people—forty-eight officials and fifty-three students and attendants—left Yokohama for San Francisco on the first leg of their mission to visit the Western treaty powers. The Japanese delegation, the second to visit the United States since Matthew Perry opened Japan to the West in 1854, desired consultations with American officials on proposed revisions in their existing agreements with the United States. They wished to secure, among other things, tariff autonomy and an end to extraterritoriality, which in essence meant that all American citizens residing in Japan were not subject to Japanese laws. Iwakura's party landed in San Francisco in early January 1872 and proceeded across country via the newly opened transcontinental railroad. The Japanese delegation was warmly welcomed at numerous receptions in cities along the way, most notably in Salt Lake City, where Iwakura met the Mormon leader Brigham Young, and Chicago, where the Japanese envoys presented the mayor a donation of $5,000 to aid the victims of the city's recent Great Fire. When they arrived in Washington, President Grant hosted a formal audience, at which Ambassador Iwakura explained that he and his colleagues not only sought consultation on treaty revision, but also wished to observe and study the American system of government. "It is our purpose," he announced, "to select from the various institutions prevailing among enlightened nations such as are best suited to our present condition, and adopt them, in gradual reforms and improvements of our policy and customs, so as to be upon an equality with them."[28]

The Japanese interest in American institutions extended to the educational system. A number of the Japanese students in the Iwakura mission intended to continue their schooling in the United States, including five young women, the first Japanese females to be sent overseas for their education. Apparently, this idea originated with an imperial official who earlier had visited the United States and was impressed with the educational opportunities and general respect American women enjoyed. Japan was embarking on its own program of modernization, and literate mothers were deemed essential as the basis for the nation's future educational program. This sort of cultural and educational "borrowing" was highly flattering to American nationalists such as James G. Blaine. It was not only gratifying but also welcome confirmation of the U.S. mission to serve as a model and example to the rest of the world. As speaker of the House, Blaine took great pride in formally welcoming the Iwakura delegation to a congressional reception, later requesting from the Japanese embassy what would become a cherished memento of the occasion: a copy of the original text in Japanese of Iwakura's remarks to the House of Representatives.[29]

Two years after the visit of the Japanese mission, on December 18, 1874, in one of his last official acts as speaker, Blaine greeted another delegation that viewed the United States as a model republic and confirmed its growing status as a Pacific power. He extended greetings to King Kalakaua of the Hawaiian Islands. Kalakaua, the first Hawaiian monarch to visit the United States, came to encourage the Grant administration and the American Congress to support and ratify a Hawaiian reciprocity treaty. Prior to Kalakaua's visit, only one other Hawaiian king had gone abroad. Fifty years earlier, Kamehameha II had journeyed to Great Britain on a similar diplomatic and goodwill mission. The fact that a Hawaiian king now came to Washington instead of London symbolized a momentous shift in the focus of Hawaiian interests. Accompanying the monarch was Elisha Allen, formerly of Bangor, Maine, and known to Blaine through his wife's family, the Stanwoods of Augusta. Allen was one more link in the missionary and political chain that connected Maine to the Sandwich Islands. The fight for reciprocity was successful, but only after an article was added to the treaty that guaranteed future American hegemony in the islands, and Secretary of State Fish prophesied the treaty would "bind these islands to the United States with hoops of steel." Blaine discreetly did his part to tie Hawaii ever closer to the United States, which Allen graciously acknowledged: "For the kind interest which you have taken in our island affairs you are held in grateful remembrance."[30]

While Blaine reveled in his country's increasingly recognized status as a world power, the Maine Republican was troubled by a glaring

contradiction in America's claim to national greatness. It was an incon-
sistency that would bedevil future generations of Americans as well.
The contradiction involved racial equality and the protection of the
rights of national citizenship. The fact that Americans, white or black,
enjoyed greater privileges and protection abroad than they did in the
states of the former Confederacy was a national disgrace. The United
States protected citizenship abroad while it ignored it at home. "I do
not understand, and cannot comprehend," Blaine admitted, "how a
government that has an arm long enough and strong enough . . . to
reach over the Atlantic and beyond the Pyrenees, and take a man from
the hands of Spanish tyranny, has not power enough to reach down
into Alabama and South Carolina and protect its own citizens both
native born and naturalized." This failure, personified by outrages
against blacks and their white supporters in the South, was a blot on
America's newfound glory because "the majesty and might of a nation
are measured, fellow citizens, by no standard so accurately as by the
degree of protection given to their citizens or subjects." On the eve of
the nation's centennial celebration, Blaine's hope for racial equality and
untainted national glory, as expressed in his 1868 speech forecasting
the coming success of Grant's diplomacy, had not been achieved.[31]

When he stepped down as speaker of the House in March 1875, an
ambitious James G. Blaine, now forty-five years old, was a renowned
and famous national figure. Because of his personal charisma on the
campaign trail and his magnetism as a political orator, he became
identified in the public mind as "Mr. Republican." For many of the
party faithful, Blaine was destined to be the obvious successor to Grant
in the White House. In the decade or so since he had left the Maine
legislature for the national arena, Blaine had become a sophisticated
internationalist who favored strong executive control of the nation's
foreign policy. As speaker during the Grant years he had played an
unprecedented role in formulation of foreign policy, an honor traditionally reserved for influential members of the Senate. His imperial
blueprints were still undergoing modification, but several features of
the architecture of the future American empire were already visible.
The United States was to be the destined leader of the Western Hemisphere, with the Monroe Doctrine being the guiding principle for
a Pan-Americanism that would lead the sisterhood of American republics in the paths of peace, prosperity, and power. Overseas territorial expansion in the Pacific might prove necessary for the success of
Blaine's blueprints, but informal empire, based on economic and commercial power, remained his preferred imperial course. Ultimately as
well, Blaine's imperial vision called for Great Britain to be displaced

by the United States as the world's number one power. Over the next two decades Blaine, first as a senator and then as secretary of state, would attempt to put his blueprints into operation.

Notes

1. Garry Wills, *Lincoln at Gettysburg: The Words That Remade America* (New York: Simon and Schuster, 1992), 263.

2. Remarks of James G. Blaine, April 21, 1864, *Congressional Globe*, 38th Cong., 1st sess., part 2 (Washington, DC: 1864), 1797–1800.

3. Ibid., 1797.

4. Ibid., 1799.

5. Ibid., Remarks of Henry Winter Davis, April 4, 1864, 1408.

6. Ibid.

7. Remarks of Henry Winter Davis, December 15, 1864, *Congressional Globe*, 38th Cong., 2d sess., part 1 (Washington, DC: 1865), 48.

8. Quoted in William A. Williams, *The Roots of the Modern American Empire* (New York: Random House, 1969), 136.

9. Quoted in James G. Blaine, *Twenty Years of Congress: From Lincoln to Garfield*, 2 vols. (Norwich, CT: Henry Bill Publishing Company, 1886), 2:478–85.

10. Ibid., 476.

11. Quoted in Gail Hamilton, *Biography of James G. Blaine* (Norwich, CT: Henry Bill Publishing Company, 1895), 182–85.

12. Gaillard Hunt, *Israel, Elihu and Cadwallader Washburn: A Chapter in American Biography* (New York: Macmillan Company, 1925), 120; Blaine, *Twenty Years*, 2:192.

13. See two articles by Robert E. May, "Lobbyists for Commercial Empire: Jane Cazneau, William Cazneau, and U.S. Caribbean Policy, 1846–1878," *Pacific Historical Review* 48 (August 1979), 383–412; and "'Plenipotentiary in Petticoats': Jane M. Cazneau and American Foreign Policy in the Mid-Nineteenth Century," in *Women and American Foreign Policy: Lobbyists, Critics, and Insiders*, ed. Edward P. Crapol (Wilmington, DE: Scholarly Resources, 1992), 19–44.

14. Blaine, *Twenty Years*, 2:340. Earlier, in a July 4, 1877, speech on "The Mexican Danger," Blaine credited Seward with "the honor of being the first statesman to add to our territory on the north, as he did in the purchase of Alaska." See *The Independent*, July 12, 1877, 7.

15. Remarks of James G. Blaine, February 17, 1868, *Congressional Globe*, 40th Cong., 2d sess. (Washington, DC: 1868), 1223–24; Henry Merritt Wriston, *Executive Agents in American Foreign Relations* (Baltimore: Johns Hopkins University Press, 1929), 122–23.

16. James G. Blaine to Israel Washburn, Jr., September 12, 1867, in Hunt, *Israel Washburn*, 121.

17. Remarks of James G. Blaine, December 10, 1868, *Congressional Globe*, 40th Cong., 3d sess., part 1 (Washington, DC: 1869), 58.

18. Ibid.

19. Edward P. Crapol, *America for Americans: Economic Nationalism and Anglophobia in the Late Nineteenth Century* (Westport, CT: Greenwood Press, 1973), 22–24; Alexander Del Mar, "Henry C. Carey's Roundtable I," *Gunton's Magazine* 13 (August 1897), 99–108.

20. Lindley M. Keasbey, *The Nicaragua Canal and the Monroe Doctrine* (New York: G. P. Putnam's Sons, 1896), 314–15; David McCullough, *The Path between the Seas: The Creation of the Panama Canal* (New York: Simon and Schuster, 1977), 26–28.

21. James D. Richardson, *Messages and Papers of the Presidents,* 11 vols. (Washington, DC: Bureau of National Literature and Art, 1905), 7:37; Crapol, *America for Americans,* 23–33.

22. Allan Nevins, *Hamilton Fish: The Inner History of the Grant Administration* (New York: Dodd, Mead and Company, 1937), 910.

23. James G. Blaine to Ulysses S. Grant, March 17, 1869, in *The Papers of Ulysses S. Grant,* ed. John Y. Simon, 22 vols. (Carbondale, IL: Southern Illinois University Press, 1995), 20:144.

24. Charles I. Bevans, *Treaties and Other International Agreements of the United States of America, 1776–1949,* 13 vols. (Washington, DC: Government Printing Office, 1974), 12:171, 158–59.

25. Mrs. James G. Blaine to Walker Blaine, May 1, 1872, in *Letters of Mrs. James G. Blaine,* ed. Harriet S. Blaine Beale, 2 vols. (New York: Duffield and Company, 1908), 1:123; James G. Blaine to Hamilton Fish, May 5, 1872, in Nevins, *Fish,* 542–43.

26. Blaine, *Twenty Years,* 2:493.

27. James G. Blaine to ?, January 4, 1871, in Hamilton, *Biography of Blaine,* 248.

28. Payson J. Treat, *Diplomatic Relations between the United States and Japan, 1853–1895,* 3 vols. (Stanford: Stanford University Press, 1932), 1:428.

29. Ibid., 427. A copy of the Japanese text of Iwakura's remarks is in the James G. Blaine Papers, Library of Congress.

30. Hamilton, *Biography of Blaine,* 314, 374.

31. Speech of James G. Blaine, October 28, 1874, entitled "The Democratic Party and the Constitutional Amendments," in James G. Blaine, *Political Discussions: Legislative, Diplomatic and Popular* (Norwich, CT: Henry Bill Publishing Company, 1887), 146.

3

From the House
to the Senate

We stand where we can defy her, and we are today the only power on the globe that can defy Great Britain, and we can do it with just as much dignity or just as much insolence as we choose to employ.

—James G. Blaine, 1878

The Democratic victory in the 1874 congressional elections unexpectedly altered Blaine's anticipated and preferred career path. For the first time since before the Civil War, the Democrats won control of the House of Representatives, securing a total of 169 seats to 109 for the Republicans. While the GOP retained control of the Senate, the loss of the House meant an end to Blaine's reign as speaker. Two important changes occurred in the Maine Republican's thinking and behavior after he was ousted. First, he recklessly gave in to his presidential ambitions, succumbing to what veteran politicians then and now knowingly have labeled either the irrepressible "fire in the belly" or an attack of "presidential fever." Second, in the midst of the severe depression that gripped the nation in the mid-1870s, Blaine revamped and fine-tuned his thinking about what ailed the American economy, what governmental actions promoting overseas markets were necessary to restore and sustain economic growth and prosperity, and how foreign policy issues might be used to restore GOP success at the polls. Of the two changes, the latter was more important to the maturation of his expansionist outlook and refinement of his imperial blueprints.

Given a choice in the matter, Blaine without question would have opted to remain as speaker of the House in the

nation's centennial year and to stage a well-planned, carefully orches-
trated run at the presidency from this power base in the lower body of
Congress. But he was forced to adjust his tactics to serve his ambitions.
As a member of the House minority, the former speaker found himself
on the defensive. In order to regain the strategic initiative in the campaign of 1876, Blaine took great risks, becoming a high stakes poker
player who gambled big and narrowly lost. And although he later received the party's nomination in 1884, by all accounts 1876 was the
only time Blaine desperately wanted and unequivocally sought the
presidency. As a result of his bruising loss to Rutherford B. Hayes at
the GOP convention that year, he became more philosophical about
seeking the nation's highest office. Blaine essentially adopted a take-it-
or-leave-it attitude, probably recognizing, if not always following, the
wisdom of his wife's telling comment after the assassination of
James A. Garfield in 1881: "This election of a president every four years
makes life very short. Hayes is elected, and the disappointed immediately mortgage the future. And Garfield dies, and his friends, pushed
to the wall, at once forecast conclusions for the next administration."[1]

As the centennial year approached, the Republicans knew they
were in trouble. The scandals of the Grant years had alienated many
Americans. To regain the moral high ground for his party and to kick
off his presidential campaign, James G. Blaine introduced a joint resolution at the opening of the Forty-fourth Congress in December 1875,
proposing what he hoped would be a popular and politically expedient amendment to the Constitution. The Blaine amendment, as it was
commonly known, would prevent states from enacting "any law re-
specting an establishment of religion or prohibiting the free exercise
thereof" and would forbid the expenditure of public money for private
or religious schools. President Grant had prepared the way for the
amendment in his annual message, which had been presented to Congress a week earlier, by recommending the separation of church and
state in public education. Because he offered the formal bill to the
House, Blaine appeared to be the Grant administration's anointed candidate for the Republican nomination. Few among the American public were fooled by the lofty rhetoric urging support of the measure. The
Blaine amendment immediately was seen for what it was, a blatant
political maneuver to restore the Republicans as the reform party
among the nation's Protestants, especially those in Northern cities who
felt threatened by the encroachments of Catholic immigrants. This proposed sixteenth amendment never emerged from Congress; although
approved by the House, it was defeated in the Senate. No matter, it

served Blaine's purposes in polarizing the public and drawing the Republican faithful tightly around the party banner.

The public education controversy proved but a warm-up for the main event. Blaine's real blockbuster came on January 10, 1876, when he ignited what would be one of the most bitter debates in the history of the House of Representatives. Among the Democrats elected to Congress in 1874 were a number of ex-Confederate army officers, at least sixty of whom had held the rank of brigadier general or higher. Dubbed "rebel brigadiers" by alarmed Republicans such as Blaine, these men were in the vanguard of support for a Democratic bill to grant amnesty to about 750 remaining Confederate leaders who had not been pardoned. Blaine surprised the majority of his House colleagues and many of the general public by offering an amendment that excluded Jefferson Davis from pardon. Blaine held the former president of the Confederacy responsible for the horrors of Andersonville, a prisoner-of-war camp in Georgia where scores of Union soldiers suffered and died. Again, Blaine succeeded in polarizing the American people with his most recent "bloody shirt" attack. It too was another transparent political sideshow, considering that the Republicans, just a few years earlier when they held the majority in the House and Blaine was Speaker, had introduced virtually identical amnesty legislation. True, it had not been a top priority for Republicans and had died in committee, but the intent had been there for all to see.

Both of these carefully calculated moves kept Blaine in the public eye and made him even more of a hero to the Republican rank and file, especially veterans of the Grand Army of the Republic. But for some of his friends, the attack on Jefferson Davis and the opening of old sectional wounds at the beginning of the centennial year seemed reckless and out of character for such an astute and experienced politician. James A. Garfield, although a chief Blaine ally in the House debate, was one Republican who displayed a measure of magnanimity to his Southern colleagues. The Ohio congressman confided to a friend that "Blaine made a very powerful speech but lost his temper and some reputation." When Blaine went on the attack again on the day the debate was concluded, Garfield conceded the speech was "full of strong and brilliant points" but his friend failed "in maintaining the equanimity of his temper and I think lost something by being aggressively personal."[2]

The Democratic amnesty proposal failed passage in the heat of the 1876 election campaign. Blaine had succeeded in torpedoing it. Two decades later, at the time of the Spanish-American War in 1898, after

Jefferson Davis had died, full amnesty was granted to surviving Confederate soldiers. Finally, in October 1978, one hundred thirteen years after Lee's surrender at Appomattox and more than a century after James G. Blaine blocked the centennial year amnesty effort, President Jimmy Carter of Georgia, proud Southerner and dedicated advocate of civil rights for all Americans, restored Davis's citizenship, saying the leader of the ill-fated Confederacy "should no longer be singled out for punishment." But there never has been a pardon for Jefferson Davis.[3]

Conventional wisdom at the time saw the next episode in Blaine's 1876 political odyssey as a payback by defeated and angry Southern Democrats, the "rebel brigadiers," for his ruthless assault on the former Confederate president. Just as the Maine Republican seemed assured of his party's nomination at their June convention in Cincinnati, Ohio, a scandal broke that crippled his candidacy and morally tainted him for life. It was charged in the press that Blaine, while speaker of the House, had been on the take and in the service of railroad interests. A Congressional investigation ensued, led by his Southern enemies. One James Mulligan came forward claiming he possessed letters written by Blaine that proved his guilt. But before these "Mulligan letters" could be entered as evidence to the House committee, Blaine retrieved them from his antagonist under dubious circumstances on the justification that the letters were private and his personal property. At this point Blaine appeared to have lost his moral compass. For many among the American public, this high-handed and desperate action—blatantly "stealing" the letters from Mulligan—incriminated Blaine even without their knowing the full content of the correspondence.

The melodrama continued. After gaining possession of the letters, Blaine dramatically appeared to vindicate himself by giving an incredible performance on the House floor in which he selectively read from the correspondence before the investigating committee and packed spectator galleries. Under this intense pressure Blaine almost cracked completely. One Sunday morning in early June he collapsed at the doorway of his church, physically and emotionally spent. By now his critics had become so cynical that the next day one newspaper headline announced "Blaine feigns a faint." Perhaps some journalists knew the man only too well. In his diary for June 14, 1876, Secretary of State Hamilton Fish privately recorded the following scenario. After his recovery from the swoon at the church and to prove he was on the mend, Blaine sent his son Walker to inquire if Fish would take a carriage ride with his father. Hesitantly, Fish agreed and recorded: "We took the drive, Mr. Blaine indicating the streets through which we should pass." The news of Blaine's carriage ride was telegraphed to Cincinnati where the Republican convention was in session and, according to Fish, "produced great enthusiasm among his friends."[4]

To a degree the theatrics and public posturing were successful. True, he failed to receive the coveted prize of the Republican presidential nomination, but Blaine survived politically and the charges of corruption were never proven. Legions of his loyal followers, including such party luminaries as future Secretary of State John Hay, thought he was innocent of all wrongdoing. Perhaps he was innocent. Nonetheless, James G. Blaine never totally overcame the stigma of political corruption. Many of his fellow Americans at the time thought he was guilty, morally bankrupt, and a shameless rogue to boot. Ever after this incident, Blaine would be tainted with the odor of corruption, and political cartoonists had a field day casting him as the "tattooed man," each tattoo on his body depicting an incident of alleged political malfeasance.

The publication of the "Mulligan letters" led his political enemies to taunt him in future campaigns with the mocking chant taken from the closing of one of the letters: "Kind regards to Mrs. Fisher. Burn this letter." What Blaine suspected, but the public-at-large did not know at the time, was that his misfortunes were not primarily the work of revengeful Southern Democrats. He had been undone by powerful enemies within his own party. Walter Q. Gresham, an Indiana Republican and federal judge who despised Blaine, leaked the information on the shady railroad deals and "set in motion the chain of events leading to the discovery of the famous Mulligan letters." Roscoe Conkling of New York, an aggrieved arch-rival from earlier days in the House, never forgave Blaine for describing him as having a "turkey gobbler strut" and worked assiduously both before and during the convention to deny his hated foe the party's nomination.[5]

Although unsuccessful in his bid for the presidency in 1876, Blaine in the summer of that year was elevated by the Maine state legislature to the United States Senate. For the next five years he served in the upper branch of Congress as the junior senator from Maine. From that power base and in response to the severe economic depression of the 1870s, he finalized his blueprints for American empire. Despite the damage done by the allegations that he was politically corrupt and in the pay of railroad barons, Blaine remained the ablest, most charismatic, and farsighted leader the Republican party had in the Gilded Age. After the 1876 convention, he frequently was hailed as the "Plumed Knight," in homage to the powerful nominating speech of Robert Ingersoll that used the chivalrous and brave imagery of knighthood to depict Blaine at work in Congress. The Maine Republican was a clear and incisive thinker who sustained a love affair with the American people because he appealed to their national pride and sense of destiny. As the United States entered its second century, Blaine conveyed to the general public an understanding that national greatness would be based on the twin economic pillars of America's unrivaled agricultural and industrial production. The path to national greatness would come in stages, with agricultural exports, ultimately to be joined by exports of manufactures, leading the way in establishing the United States as a major player in the international marketplace.

Blaine also understood that there was a downside to the United States' phenomenal productive capacity in the post–Civil War era. Overproduction became a major source of the nation's economic woes. Surplus products from farm and factory glutted the home market, leading to an economic downturn marked by lower prices, widespread unemployment, and social unrest. A sense of urgency prevailed as the Maine Republican increasingly came to see the expansion of foreign markets as the way to guarantee economic prosperity and social peace. In his earlier thinking, overseas economic expansion was a necessary prerequisite to national greatness; in the context of the depression of the 1870s, Blaine came to believe overseas markets were not only necessary but essential to the preservation of the American system. On the basis of his most recent analysis, Blaine confidently forecast that the "farmers of the Republic will control its destiny." And in keeping with his faith that American industry would someday come to dominate world markets, he also believed that American global prestige was assured because "we are one of the foremost manufacturing nations in the world; we have pushed population away beyond what but yesterday seemed the most distant frontier or indeed there is no frontier left save that which is washed by the waves of either great ocean." Of course, for Blaine the ocean frontiers of preference washed the shores of Latin America and Asia.[6]

The effects of the severe business dislocation and economic depression of the 1870s dramatized for Blaine—as it did for other American leaders, including President Rutherford B. Hayes, Secretary of State William M. Evarts, and Congressman James A. Garfield—the problem of overproduction and the need for new markets to absorb the surplus of U.S. farms and factories. Blaine readily grasped the eventual importance of agricultural exports in generating recovery from the depression and this perception structured and shaped his imperial blueprints about the role of exports in the future success of the United States. Agricultural exports of cotton, wheat, and meat products, which comprised 78 percent of all domestic exports in 1879, 83 percent in 1880, and 82 percent in 1881, not only helped restore economic recovery from one of the worst depressions in the country's history but also created the necessary foreign exchange and capital to sustain and promote further industrialization. These export statistics may be mundane economic data for Americans today, but for Blaine and countless numbers of his contemporaries, they were a source of pride and lay at the heart of his and their dreams of empire and a glorious national destiny.

As a freshman senator, Blaine chose Latin America as one of the geographic areas to highlight in the reformulation and refinement of his blueprints. During the winter of 1877–1878 he studied and evaluated the resources, needs, and possibilities of the Southern Hemisphere. He was aided in his research by his old Maine buddy, John L. Stevens, who had served as American minister to Paraguay and Uruguay from 1870 to 1874. His former editorial partner, who recently had been appointed by the incoming Hayes administration as minister to Norway and Sweden, kept Blaine informed about trade prospects in Latin America and the obstacles American exporters might face in capturing those markets. Another source of information was James A. Garfield, his political as well as intellectual ally. Garfield clearly recognized the problems involved and recommended that the United States build an infrastructure in support of expanded hemispheric trade. In February 1876, that tumultuous year of partisan bickering and political bloodletting, the Ohio representative had denounced an attempt by the Democrats to cut the diplomatic and consular appropriation. Reducing the number of the nation's missions abroad would be self-defeating and virtual commercial suicide for the United States in South America and in Japan and China. "Will we wonder," Garfield asked his colleagues, "if this be done, that Great Britain gets the control of those countries away from us?" The end result of gutting the appropriation, Garfield predicted, would be to "abandon the field to Great Britain."[7]

The initial phase of Senator Blaine's Pan-American policy appeared in the spring of 1878 during the second session of the Forty-fifth Congress, and it centered on his efforts to provide a federal subsidy for an American steamship line to Brazil. During the previous winter, when he had evaluated the commercial resources of the Latin American nations with an eye to increasing American trade at the expense of European competitors, Blaine had become particularly interested in Brazil. That attraction may have been influenced initially by the 1876 visit to the United States of Dom Pedro, the emperor of Brazil. The emperor was keen to develop closer commercial ties with his northern neighbor and, as a first step, offered to create an annual subsidy to help establish a steam line service between Brazil and the United States. Shortly after the emperor returned to Brazil, the entrepreneur and shipbuilder John Roach negotiated a contract with the Brazilian government that pledged a subsidy of $125,000 to create a steamship service between the two countries, providing the American government pledged the same amount.

Blaine vigorously supported the Roach subsidy in the Senate, which led to charges of political corruption from his ever-alert opponents. It was known that in past campaigns the shipbuilder had been a generous financial supporter of the Plumed Knight. But in this case, neither Blaine's imperial blueprints nor his hemispheric program can be understood simply in terms of political favoritism or the influence of a special interest group. As part of his larger policy, Blaine believed federal support for the Roach steamship line with the South American monarchy was the necessary first step to inaugurate his overall program for commercial expansion in the hemisphere. Brazil was an untapped market for American agricultural products and industrial goods. The problem, as he explained to his Senate colleagues, was that "they do not know in Brazil what we have to sell—what we are able to manufacture and really offer them." As a result, the United States lost sales to this market when Brazil purchased its butter and cheese, its boots and shoes, and its agricultural implements from Europe.[8]

The prevailing trade balance between the United States and Brazil was highly unfavorable to the North American republic and reflected the generally weak position of American commerce with Latin American countries in the last third of the nineteenth century. The trade pattern with Brazil, in which the United States was a heavy importer of Brazilian raw materials and agricultural goods while its exports to that nation were negligible, represented one concrete example of the deficits and deficiencies of American hemispheric commerce that a number of Blaine's contemporaries recognized. Secretary of State Evarts, for example, concluded that until Congress inaugurated "a system of steam communication equal to that of England and France," American businessmen would be unable to compete profitably in Latin American markets. Senator Blaine believed there were several reasons for the unequal features of hemispheric trade. Over the course of the next ten to fifteen years, he would offer a variety of solutions, but in the case of Brazil he emphasized the need for regular steamship service between the two countries.

There was an added embarrassment to American national pride in the pattern of trade with Brazil. Because its shipping facilities to Brazil were virtually nonexistent, the United States depended to a great extent upon British lines for its communication with the South American country. This arrangement decidedly favored British merchants and traders. A triangular trade existed that had colonial overtones for Americans: Brazilian exports of sugar and coffee were transported in British vessels to the eastern ports of the United States; after unloading the agricultural and semiprocessed products of Brazil and perhaps taking on some American manufactured goods and foodstuffs, including wheat and flour, the ship would depart for Great Britain; only after unloading and reloading in a British port did the ship embark on a return voyage to Brazil.

It was painfully apparent to Blaine that American commercial interests suffered as a result of this inequitable trading pattern. On the one hand, American merchants and manufacturers had to pay the additional freight entailed in shipping to Brazil via Great Britain. On the other hand, American manufacturers somehow had to remain competitive with British goods shipped at lower rates and delivered with less elapsed time. British merchants thus possessed a clear advantage in the Brazilian market and British shipping lines made profits from American commerce with Brazil. Blaine argued for the necessity of establishing an American steamship service to Brazil in order to end the British monopoly. As a first step in this effort to gain control of additional Latin American markets, Blaine favored a federal subsidy for John Roach's line to Brazil.

Under the Maine Republican's persistent guidance the subsidy bill passed in the Senate. In the House of Representatives it met stiff resistance and, after acrimonious debate that included charges of political corruption and cries of "jobbery for Roach," was soundly defeated. A number of House members questioned the viability and effectiveness of government subsidies for steamship routes, particularly in light of the failure of several earlier federal efforts to fund a line in the Pacific. Blaine was undaunted by the defeat of the Roach subsidy bill; he would energetically pursue other means to achieve his goal of American political and economic hegemony in the hemisphere. In fact, the debate over the proposed subsidy measure had provided him the opportunity once again to alert the American public to the challenges to their nation's destiny posed by Britain's domination of the world's oceans. For Blaine, breaking the British grip on Brazilian trade was only the opening volley in a battle for the carrying trade of the world.

In the decade or so since the Civil War, the United States had allowed its merchant marine to deteriorate into a deplorable condition.

It was not surprising that, as a Senator from a major shipbuilding state, Blaine sought to restore America's merchant marine to its former glory. He feared that if the task were not undertaken by the federal government it would be tantamount to saying to Great Britain, "take the seas, they are yours," with the end result that the United States would again "become tributary to Great Britain." But he also believed that America was "today the only power on the globe that can defy Great Britain." To challenge British supremacy by rebuilding the nation's merchant marine, Blaine advocated reliance on the traditional navigation laws of the United States; it was his objective to foster a broad program of federal support based on the assumption that America had the right to control and carry its commerce. He reasoned that if American agricultural exports went to Europe in American vessels at least one link in Great Britain's chain of control on the world's oceans would be shattered.[9]

The Congressional stalemate that defeated the Roach subsidy bill doomed as well any legislation to aid the restoration of the merchant marine, which ensured the continued decline of American shipping in the 1880s. In the Senate debate on these maritime issues, Blaine revealed that his thinking about the former mother country was marked by a certain ambivalence. His rhetoric may have been hostile and critical, but along with many other late nineteenth-century American Anglophobes, he expressed a grudging admiration for Great Britain's global economic preeminence. Blaine viewed Britain's mercantile and maritime policies as a successful and proven approach that the United States wisely might emulate. The senator candidly admitted that a nation could always learn from its rivals, and he believed that the worldwide competition with Britain for markets and trade offered no exception to that historical rule. Blaine frequently interpreted Great Britain's supremacy as the result of a strategy similar to his own program for national greatness. The defeat of his proposals to establish America's maritime independence simply motivated him to expand his program for hegemony in Latin America into a more coherent and integrated set of policies. The blueprints for most of the policies of this integrated program were complete by 1881 when Blaine briefly served as secretary of state under Garfield.

Unlike a number of other economic expansionists in this period, Blaine did not jump on board the free silver bandwagon. The free silver campaign, which contained more than a touch of quackery and irrationality, promoted the idea that the remonetization of silver would open markets for American exports in Central and South America. And although the debate over what form of currency would best aid the nation's overseas economic expansion was accompanied by an emotional commitment that frequently verged on the fanatical, the "silverites" and their agrarian supporters did present a plausible analysis of how the remonetization of the white metal would alleviate the nation's economic distress. No matter, because James G. Blaine and other gold standard advocates would have none of it. They feared a free silver policy would devalue the nation's currency, making it even more difficult for American exporters to compete with the British in foreign markets. In Blaine's eyes, a country with a currency based on silver was a second-class nation. Consequently, he believed it was necessary for the United States to retain the gold standard and remain with the gold system in order to overpower Great Britain in the markets of Latin America and Asia. He flatly rejected the silver panacea for capturing hemispheric trade; the gold standard was the monetary system best suited to Blaine's emerging Pan-Americanism.

Another modification in Blaine's blueprints came with his gradual acceptance of reciprocity as a tactic for overseas economic expansion. As a method to open markets and increase trade, a policy of reciprocity involved employing the treaty-making power of the executive branch to lower tariff duties selectively on a country-to-country basis. For example, a bilateral agreement between the United States and Mexico might be negotiated in which Washington would reduce its duties on a list of specified products imported from Mexico in return for a similar lowering of Mexican duties on goods imported from the United States. These reductions were to be established on a quid pro quo basis with each nation receiving comparable benefits as part of the process of lowering tariff duties. If implemented with a most-favored-nation provision that extended the same benefits to other countries having treaties with either party, it was assumed that the general flow of international commerce would be enhanced. Consequently, nineteenth-century Americans traditionally viewed the tactic of reciprocity as a free trade device designed to lower tariff rates and undermine protectionism.

Accepting the logic of the reciprocity tactic was not an easy or a quick decision for someone like Blaine. First, he was a lifelong protectionist who abhorred any tampering with that principle and opposed calls for tariff reform or revision, and he identified reciprocity as a free trade policy that ultimately might lead to the demise of protectionism. A protective tariff was designed to overcome foreign domination of American economic development, and, in his view, a high tariff policy had facilitated the nation's rapid industrialization after the Civil War. Protection also had enabled American industry to capture a greater share of the domestic market, usually at the expense of British manufacturers. In the eyes of Republicans like Blaine the protective tariff had accomplished its major goal by securing the home market for American manufactures. Blaine, for one, was loath to tamper with success and in 1878 offered several Senate resolutions opposing any radical alteration of the tariff. There was, he argued in May 1878, "no more hurtful agitation today in this country than the agitation of the tariff," primarily because it would delay recovery from the depression and retard the return of prosperity.[10]

The second reason Blaine had doubts about reciprocity as a policy stemmed from his negative reaction to an earlier, unsuccessful reciprocity treaty with Canada. In force from 1854 to 1866, it had not obtained the promised benefits for American producers and consumers. Instead of drawing the territories of British North America closer to the United States, as its supporters had predicted, the treaty had strengthened the Canadians and contributed to the movement that led to the creation of the Dominion of Canada in 1867. In Blaine's view, farmers and exporters in his home state of Maine had been the victims of this ill-advised policy of reciprocity. "There was scarcely a product on the list which could be exported from the United States to Canada without loss," he later recalled, "while the great market of the United States was thrown open to Canada without tax or charge for nearly everything which she could produce." The entire arrangement was designed "almost wholly to favor Canadian interests." To avoid another unequal commercial treaty of this sort, Blaine in the summer of 1874 kicked off what would be his last campaign for Congress by promising his constituents that he flatly would oppose any future calls for a reciprocity agreement with Canada.[11]

Blaine's third objection to reciprocity treaties involved constitutional issues and the separation of powers between the legislative and executive branches of the federal government. In the opening speech of his 1874 race for Congress, Blaine not only denounced the earlier treaty with Canada but also clearly explained his constitutional objections to the reciprocity principle. He was against "the whole policy of adjusting revenue questions by the treaty-making power," and expressed his desire "to enter on behalf of my constituents an emphatic protest. The Constitution gives to the House of Representatives the sole and exclusive right to originate Bills of Revenue, and this great power should be kept where it can be controlled by the direct and unbiased vote of the people." Blaine's thinking on reciprocity undoubtedly was influenced by Justin Morrill of Vermont, who adamantly opposed the "humbug" of reciprocity treaties. Morrill, who had toured

Europe with Blaine in 1867, moved from the House to the Senate that year where he served on the Senate Finance Committee for three decades. For twenty-two years as chair of that major tariff-writing committee, Senator Morrill used every opportunity to block reciprocal tariff cutting. But in the end Morrill was deserted by several of his key allies, including his fellow New Englander Blaine who became a leading advocate of reciprocity agreements, especially with Hawaii and the countries of Latin America.[12]

When and why did James G. Blaine change his mind on reciprocity? It is difficult to say with certainty, but he probably made the shift in the late 1870s because the principle and practice of reciprocity now fit into his revised imperial blueprints. He had come to accept the argument that the overall benefits of reciprocity treaties overrode any specific objections; diplomatic objectives and his comprehensive global strategy became more important than concern for localized economic interests. After the export boom of the late 1870s, Blaine no doubt also understood that reciprocity treaties appealed to farmers and agricultural businessmen as a means of expanding their foreign markets. Additionally, the reciprocity tactic offered a way to overcome Britain's transportation and credit advantages within the hemisphere and to open the door for the American manufacturer, including the southern cotton textile producer, to establish American commercial hegemony in Latin American markets. Finally, Blaine had been educated by his peers that in cases such as Hawaiian reciprocity it was better to sacrifice immediate economic and commercial gains for political and strategic advantages that over the long haul would make the island archipelago a commercial dependency bound to the United States "by hoops of steel," in the memorable words of Secretary of State Hamilton Fish.

One facet of Blaine's outlook that did not change in this process of blueprint modification during the depression of the 1870s was his antipathy to territorial expansion south of the Rio Grande. As a partisan politician, he also remained addicted to using any occasion to "wave the bloody shirt" and castigate the South for its antebellum record of pro-slavery expansionism. Amid festive red, white, and blue garlands, patriotic music, and fireworks at Roseland Park in Woodstock, Connecticut, on the Fourth of July in 1877, the senator from Maine gave a rousing address celebrating the nation's independence and expressing anew his concerns about the South's designs on Mexican territory. This time the danger lurked in the Southwest, arising from calls by Texans for retaliation for Mexican incursions across the border into American territory. In an overly alarmist reaction, Blaine charged that this was an agitation "that menaces possibly great danger to the future of the Republic." Admittedly, at the moment the threat was slight, but the "inevitable drift of events" might "be toward the absorption by this country of a large portion of the present Republic of Mexico."

In a remarkable throwback to Northern fears about antebellum Southern expansionism, Blaine conjured up old ghosts and anxieties. He made the hackneyed charge that, although highly improbable, future territorial acquisitions in Mexico would increase the power of the Southern states in the Union. Sounding another old refrain, he accused Presidents John Tyler and James K. Polk, both Southern slaveholders, of sectional skullduggery in the 1840s by giving away territory in the Northeast and Northwest that would have strengthened nonslave-holding, free labor states in particular and the Union in general. "There can be no doubt," Blaine claimed, "that the overwhelming majority of the people of the country, and especially of the North, are hostile to further annexation of Southern territory. This was plainly shown when Mr. Seward's proposed purchase of the island of St. Thomas was peremptorily rejected; and still later when Gen. Grant's very earnest advocacy of the San Domingo scheme utterly failed to secure support even at a time when his administration was peculiarly powerful and influential in shaping measures and directing policies." On this point, the Maine senator's remarks were entirely consistent with his post–Civil War record of opposition to Caribbean expansion.

The only exception Blaine made to this basic stricture against future territorial expansion was Canada. As he had in the fight for a Constitutional amendment banning religion in public schools, Blaine appealed to the white Protestant majority in racial- and gender-coded terms when justifying this exception to his general rule of anti-expansionism. His argument was couched as well in the Whiggish antebellum tradition commonly identified with statesmen such as William H. Seward. Unlike Mexicans, who Blaine considered a "mongrel breed," the people of British North America were acceptable for admission to the Union. "No manlier, stronger, abler, better portion of the Anglo-Saxon race can be found on the globe than those who inhabit the Dominion of Canada." Blaine acknowledged that no ground-swell of public enthusiasm for annexation to the United States existed north of the border, but he avowed "that the incorporation of the British American Provinces in our Union would be a vast addition to our strength and a large element added to our growth and prosperity."[13]

The ultimate message of this highly partisan Fourth of July oration was clear. The South should not control the Union. No concession for territorial expansion south of the border was to be granted. By virtue of the victory in the Civil War, Republicans were entitled to be in control of the national government. The men in blue who died in battle and those intrepid Republican leaders who saved the Union should govern it. If white Southerners were willing to accept the party of Lincoln, then they too could be among the governing class. Blaine ended this extraordinary speech by waving the stars and stripes instead of the bloody shirt. He made a patriotic appeal to the unifying bond of national destiny: "I would include all sections in the folds of a common patriotism, inspired by a single aim, warmed by the same traditions, stimulated by like pride, looking forward to one destiny." After happily observing the country's 101st birthday with this patriotic genuflection to national greatness and glory, Senator Blaine sat down amid hearty cheers and applause from the audience. Although Blaine dutifully and repeatedly paid homage to the ideal of one destiny for the American people, these tributes rang hollow for some Americans. Among his detractors were journalists and Democratic opponents who criticized Blaine for his polarizing rhetoric and exclusionist language.

Certainly when it came to the question of the Chinese on the West Coast, his critics had a point. Senator Blaine was in the forefront of the movement to exclude further Chinese immigration to the United States. On the basis of a treaty with China in 1868—named the Burlingame Treaty for Anson Burlingame, the chief negotiator for the Chinese empire—free entry of Chinese to the United States was permitted. Over the next decade, thousands of Chinese laborers, known as "coolies," flocked to the Pacific coast states, many under contract to work on the construction of the Central Pacific Railroad. By the late 1870s more than 130,000 Chinese were residing in California, Oregon, and Nevada. In response, a virulent anti-Chinese movement arose that demanded an end to further immigration. In early 1879 a Chinese exclusion bill handily passed in the House of Representatives. In the Senate, James G. Blaine championed the exclusion law on behalf of American labor. To protect the American workingman from cheap Asian coolie labor, he vigorously defended the exclusion legislation, making the dubious charge in floor debate that because most of the Chinese had come involuntarily as contract laborers, the United States was morally and legally justified in unilaterally suspending the 1868 treaty without China's prior consent.

The struggle in the Senate over Chinese exclusion found two old friends on opposite sides of the issue. Hannibal Hamlin, Lincoln's first vice president and now the senior senator from Maine and chair of the Foreign Relations Committee, disagreed with Blaine, his longtime ally, on this issue and opposed the Chinese exclusion bill as a matter of diplomatic honor and respect for treaty obligations. Hamlin dismissed the argument that one party to a treaty could change any part of the agreement without the consent of the other as "a proposition so absurd that it would be folly to argue it." The United States had the power to do so if it chose, but Hamlin urged the Senate and the nation to follow the rule of right and not of might. Blaine's position prevailed as the Senate passed the legislation by a vote of thirty-nine ayes to twenty-seven nays. When the bill reached the White House, President Hayes vetoed it, agreeing with Senator Hamlin that the legislation violated national honor. Hayes promptly sent a commission to China to negotiate a new treaty restricting, but not prohibiting, immigration, which was ratified by the Senate shortly after Blaine resigned to head the State Department. Then, in 1882 Congress passed legislation, frequently labelled the Chinese Exclusion Act, which suspended Chinese immigration to the United States for ten years.[14]

Blaine remained an advocate of exclusion for the rest of his public and private life. His hard-line anti-Chinese stance, which had racist overtones and was at variance with his liberal support of equal rights for African Americans, dismayed some of his loyal supporters. The famous abolitionist William Lloyd Garrison took him to task in the pages of the *New York Tribune;* James A. Garfield believed Blaine had made "a great mistake in his advocacy of it"; and others saw the "presidential fever" at work again with the Plumed Knight gearing up for the 1880 campaign. Blaine was unmoved by the criticism and neither appeals to Christian brotherhood nor concerns about possible damage to trade with China altered his position against Chinese immigration. He believed his Christian duty began at home in defense of the American worker and his family. Also, in this instance, maintaining the standard of living of the American workingman by protecting him from the "illegitimate advantage" of cheap Chinese labor outweighed the future importance of the China market.

Perhaps another explanation for Blaine's strong anti-Chinese feelings may be provided in the context of the connection between his Anglo-Saxonism and his sense of American mission. Blaine believed that in order for the United States to achieve national greatness, Anglo-Saxons had to be the dominant ethnic element in American society. That meant that "either the Anglo-Saxon race will possess the Pacific slope or the Mongolians will possess it." His hostility to additional Chinese settlement in the West was consistent with his earlier opposition on racial grounds to incorporating any additional Mexican territory into the Union because of its unacceptable racially mixed population. The American mission was presumed to be synonymous with an Anglo-Saxon mission. Appealing to the exaggerated threat of a "yellow peril" engulfing the republic, Blaine offered his fellow Americans a clear, stark choice for the future: "We have this day to choose whether we will have for the Pacific coast the civilization of Christ or the civilization of Confucius."[15]

Equating American national greatness and mission with Anglo-Saxonism seemed a contradiction in terms for someone as openly anti-British as James G. Blaine. How could he square the circle by being both an outspoken Anglophobe and a proud devotee of Anglo-Saxonism? The simple answer was that Blaine saw no contradiction in his advocacy of both viewpoints. Along with his British counterparts, the Maine Republican believed in a racial hierarchy with Anglo-Saxons at the top because, as he had argued when favoring Canada's entry into the Union, it was apparent that Anglo-Saxons were a superior breed. He and his generation of Americans also held in common with their British cousins certain cultural perceptions, including shared Victorian attitudes toward religion and gender. Among these were a belief in the primacy of Protestant Christianity and a belief that males protected women who in turn were cherished for their moral purity. In addition, certain supposedly innate traits, biologically determined as well as culturally learned, characterized the economic and political success of English-speaking peoples: intelligence, industry, a knack for self-government, and, not the least, a swashbuckling love of adventure. Not surprisingly, a shared Anglo-Saxon adventurousness and their common pursuit of expansionist capitalism and empire made these two English-speaking nations each other's greatest commercial and imperial rival, and it was this rivalry that was at the heart of James G. Blaine's Anglophobia.

Occasionally this bond of Anglo-Saxonism was also displayed by British statesmen. The Liberal leader William E. Gladstone, who had sparked Blaine's ire during the Civil War with his remark that the South virtually had established its independence, recognized the broad cultural similarities between the two peoples in an article entitled "Kin Beyond Sea," which was published in the *North American Review* in 1878. Gladstone maintained that because the American people were basically Anglo-Saxon kin, the United States posed a serious threat to Britain's commercial preeminence. At that time Britain and the United States were the two strongest nations in the world, with the latter having created on the North American continent "the greatest continuous empire ever established by man." Gladstone's forecast for the young republic was equally laudatory: "it is she alone who, at a coming time, can and probably will, wrest from us that commercial primacy." This admission of America's mighty potential was music to Blaine's ears and welcome confirmation from an unexpected source that his vision of a glorious American destiny was attainable. No matter that Gladstone recanted on this prediction in 1881 after a firestorm of criticism at home for such heresy. His recantation was ignored across the Atlantic; for years afterward Gladstone would be quoted by American patriots who boastfully proclaimed a dawning national greatness.[16]

As the presidential year of 1880 approached, James G. Blaine was again a leading candidate for the Republican nomination. Observers may have caught a glimpse of "presidential fever" in the Plumed Knight's posturing on national greatness and the need to sustain Anglo-Saxon dominance, but this time his heart was not in the contest. He entered the fray primarily to deny former President Grant a chance at a third term and was most pleased when his beloved friend of almost twenty years, James A. Garfield, won the Republican nomination. Blaine eagerly took to the hustings after the convention to secure yet another GOP victory and a continuing lock on the White House. Although Garfield returned Blaine's friendship with genuine affection, he did not fully trust his colleague from Maine. As he confessed to his diary prior to securing the party's nomination, "I like Blaine—always have—yet there is an element in him which I distrust." Once elected, however, Garfield put aside his misgivings and offered Blaine the position of secretary of state.[17]

In 1881 some of James G. Blaine's contemporaries thought him merely a Gilded Age spoilsman who was ill prepared and ill suited to be secretary of state. Many others knew better. The Plumed Knight may have been the most partisan of domestic politicians, but he also was a sophisticated internationalist with a broad and deep knowledge of world affairs. From his time as journalist and editor in Augusta, Maine, Blaine had closely observed and mastered the key issues of American foreign relations. As a congressman, he had debated the nation's future destiny, toured Europe, and conversed with the leading statesmen of the day; as speaker of the House, he had welcomed and dined with Lord Iwakura Tomomi, head of the second Japanese delegation to visit the United States, and entertained the Hawaiian king; as senator, he fought for an expanded, rebuilt merchant marine to challenge Great Britain for control of the world's carrying trade. Early on he realized commercial expansion, not unlimited territorial expansion, was the key to hegemony. Acting on that belief, Blaine had opposed the schemes of Seward and Grant for Caribbean territorial acquisitions and instead favored a Pan-Americanism that would lead to American political and commercial hegemony in the hemisphere.

Blaine was fascinated by world events and for amusement, so the story goes, would spin the world globe in his library and contemplate the planet's future. As a leading Republican in Congress for almost two decades, he came to understand that the most hotly contested political issues of the day, particularly the tariff and currency questions, had a foreign policy as well as a domestic dimension that would shape and determine the nation's unfolding destiny. In his public addresses Blaine provided historical background for his policy prescriptions; he was a confident leader who knew where the nation had been and where it was going. As a student of the American past, he was ever alert to historical precedent and practice. For instance, it was not an uncommon exercise for him to review in detail, as he did in preparation for the debate over Chinese exclusion, the provisions of all of the nation's previous treaties and international agreements. Consequently, at the end of his senatorial career, the blueprints for an American empire were near their final form and Blaine himself was well prepared to serve as secretary of state.

Notes

1. Mrs. James G. Blaine to Margaret Blaine, Christmas Day, 1881, in *Letters of Mrs. James G. Blaine*, ed. Harriet S. Blaine Beale, 2 vols. (New York: Duffield and Company, 1908), 1:276.

2. James A. Garfield to Harmon Austin, January 16, 1876, in Theodore Clarke Smith, *The Life and Letters of James Abram Garfield*, 2 vols. (New Haven, CT: Yale University Press, 1925), 1:594–95.

3. James Ford Rhodes, *History of the United States*, 8 vols. (Port Washington, NY: Kennikat Press, Inc., 1967), 6:440–41; *Public Papers of the Presidents of the United States, Jimmy Carter, 1978* (Washington, DC: U.S. Government Printing Office, 1979), 1786.

4. Quoted in Allan Nevins, *Hamilton Fish: The Inner History of the Grant Administration* (New York: Dodd, Mead and Company, 1937), 828.

5. Charles W. Calhoun, *Gilded Age Cato: The Life of Walter Q. Gresham* (Lexington, KY: University Press of Kentucky, 1988), 48–9; Allan Peskin, *Garfield, A Biography* (Kent, OH: Kent State University Press, 1978), 398–99.

6. James G. Blaine, *Political Discussions: Legislative, Diplomatic and Popular* (Norwich, CT: Henry Bill Publishing Company, 1887), 199; an Address delivered by Hon. James G. Blaine at Oshkosh, Wisconsin, September 30, 1874, James G. Blaine Papers, Library of Congress.

7. Remarks of James A. Garfield, February 7, 1876, *Congressional Record*, 44th Cong., 1st sess., (Washington, DC: 1876), 926–28.

8. Ibid., Remarks of James G. Blaine, June 5, 1878, 45th Cong., 2nd sess., 4134.

9. Ibid.

10. Ibid., Remarks of May 1, 1878, 2996.

11. James G. Blaine, *Twenty Years of Congress: From Lincoln to Garfield*, 2 vols. (Norwich, CT: Henry Bill Publishing Company, 1886), 2:620.

12. Blaine, *Political Discussions*, 124; Alfred E. Eckes, Jr., *Opening America's Market, U.S. Foreign Trade Policy Since 1776* (Chapel Hill: University of North Carolina Press, 1995), 68.

13. Address of James G. Blaine on "The Mexican Danger," July 4, 1877, in *The Independent*, July 12, 1877. I am indebted to Charles W. Calhoun for bringing this speech to my attention.

14. Quoted in Henry Draper Hunt, *Hannibal Hamlin: Lincoln's First Vice-President* (Syracuse: Syracuse University Press, 1969), 213.

15. Remarks of James G. Blaine, February 14, 1879, *Congressional Record*, 45th Cong., 3d sess. (Washington, DC: 1879), 1300–1303.

16. William E. Gladstone, "Kin Beyond Sea," *North American Review* (September–October 1878): 180.

17. Diary entry of April 14, 1880 in *The Diary of James A. Garfield*, eds. Harry James Brown and Frederick D. Williams, 4 vols. (East Lansing, MI: Michigan State University Press, 1981), 4(1878–1881):398.

4

Secretary of State, 1881

> If there is only one chapter in my life of which I am proud, and of the complete and absolute justification of which in history I feel sure, it is that in connection with the policy laid down by the Administration of President Garfield with respect to the South American states.
> —James G. Blaine, 1882

James G. Blaine served as secretary of state for little more than nine months in 1881. In that brief span of time he set into motion a series of initiatives that reshaped the course of American foreign policy and paved the way for the nation's burst of overseas imperial expansion at the turn of the century. He articulated policies and inaugurated proposals that ultimately challenged Great Britain's global commercial supremacy, particularly in the markets of the Western Hemisphere and the Pacific. Rightly hailed as the North American leader most responsible for instigating the modern Pan-American movement that directly led to the creation of the Pan-American Union and its successor, the Organization of American States, Blaine also extended the American security perimeter to the Hawaiian Islands in the mid-Pacific. He announced as well that any interoceanic canal project must meet American specifications because it would form part of the American coastline. Theodore Roosevelt ultimately adhered to that format in his Panama venture two decades later. Finally, Secretary Blaine authorized the voyage that led to one of the United States' first entangling treaties, the 1882 agreement negotiated by Commodore Robert W. Shufeldt with the hermit nation of Korea. In less than a year, Secretary of State Blaine had launched a series of diplomatic initiatives that, when fully implemented by his successors, would establish the United States as one of the major world powers.

Blaine's first opportunity to head the State Department came about by the slimmest of electoral margins. The Republicans narrowly won the 1880 presidential election, one of the closest in American political history. In the electoral college James A. Garfield safely triumphed by the count of 214 to 155, but he won the popular ballot by fewer than 8,000 votes out of 9.2 million cast, or by less than one-tenth of 1 percent. Blaine was instrumental in forging Garfield's slim victory and ensuring that the party of Lincoln retained control of the White House. Immediately following his selection as the party's presidential candidate at the June convention in Chicago, Garfield wrote his friend Blaine to thank him for his support, graciously acknowledging that the Plumed Knight and his loyal legions were responsible for his nomination. Garfield also sought his friend's strategic and tactical advice for the fall campaign, asking for help on specific issues that would attract voter support. Blaine always gave advice freely. But he was more important to the Garfield cause in 1880 as a stump speaker, reviewing glorious parades of the party faithful and drawing huge crowds of people in a crucial vote-getting swing through the Midwest and West during the last two months before the election.

As compensation for his key role in the nomination process and the general campaign, and because he was considered by the majority of his fellow Republicans as the logical choice for the job, Blaine was invited to join President-elect Garfield's cabinet as secretary of state shortly after the election. Blaine mulled it over for several weeks and accepted the position on December 20, 1880, warmly confiding to his longtime political ally that "however much I might admire you as a statesman, I would not enter your Cabinet if I did not believe in you as a man and love you as a friend." Garfield had made a wise appointment that led to an ideal, if brief, partnership between two seasoned politicians who worked well together as intellectual equals and kindred spirits. Although Blaine may have been drafting a set of imperial blueprints for more than a decade, Garfield was not far behind in crafting his own plans for national destiny and global power. The new chief executive shared the commitment to overseas commercial expansion and the search for foreign markets for the nation's surplus goods. In fact, the importance of reciprocity as an expansionist trade tactic was apparent to Garfield early on. He had championed the 1875 Hawaiian reciprocity treaty on the floor of the House of Representatives and probably became an advocate of reciprocal trade agreements before Blaine did. They both feared Britain's world economic power and the threat of a British commercial monopoly, especially in the Western Hemisphere and on the Pacific Rim. But Garfield was not the visceral

Anglophobe that his secretary of state was. The president-elect calmly urged a Pan-Americanist approach in Central and South America and was confident that in the Pacific the United States was slated to become "the arbiter of that sea, the controller of its commerce and chief nation that inhabits its shores."[1]

Garfield and Blaine were kindred spirits as well on overall political strategy for the new administration. Being consummate politicians, they began planning immediately for Garfield's reelection in 1884. Analyzing the breakdown of the 1880 voting patterns, they quickly realized Republicans could win future national contests without the South. For the GOP to count the South out in upcoming elections was a risky proposition, so as a safeguard Garfield and Blaine devised a two-pronged political strategy that not only dovetailed nicely with their foreign policy goals but also was designed to guarantee Republican control of the White House for a full eight years. First, they understood that the farmers and agrarian businessmen of the Midwest were a crucial element of the political formula to restore control of both elected branches of the national government to the Republicans. Second, while they intended to sustain their allegiance to black voters in the South and had no intention of jettisoning African-Americans from the GOP fold, Garfield and Blaine sought to build Republican strength among white Southerners by appealing to their growing interest in overseas market expansion for cotton textiles. Secretary of State Blaine bore major responsibility for pursuing implementation of the plan, confronting the nearly impossible task of trying to promote Negro suffrage at the same time the administration appealed for support among white voters in the South. Arguably, this Southern strategy failed on both counts.

In an extended correspondence between the two men before they took control of U.S. foreign policy in 1881, Blaine told Garfield, "When you take the nine Republican States that begin with Ohio and end with Kansas, you have the very heart of the Republican party." To guarantee continued Republican domination of that political heartland, both men agreed it was necessary to respond to the pressing demands of that region for overseas market expansion. At the top of their list of proposals to open foreign markets was a policy of reciprocity aimed at the countries of Latin America. Arthur L. Conger, a manufacturer of farm machinery and Ohio member of the Republican National Committee, described some years later a meeting he had with Blaine shortly after Garfield's death. According to Conger, both leaders believed a series of reciprocity treaties coupled with protection would benefit "the American people, and especially our manufacturers, our laboring men, and the American farmers," because "it would provide an additional market for American cereals, American beef and pork, and American farm machinery, etc." Conger also recalled Blaine saying that a Pan-American congress was part of the president's agenda and, had Garfield lived, such a hemispheric gathering would have been held during his administration. In private correspondence in late 1881, Sir Lionel Sackville-West, the British minister to the United States, confirmed the essence of Conger's account of the Garfield-Blaine strategy when he wrote his chief, Foreign Secretary Lord Granville, in London that "it may be that the Republicans are preparing theirs by propounding the policy of sole supremacy over South America—a policy which certainly is likely to be popular among the constituencies."[2]

The Southern-oriented feature of the overall strategy came about as a result of Blaine's growing realization that a number of the white ruling elite in the post-Reconstruction South were keenly interested in overseas commercial expansion. This was particularly true of two Democratic senators, Lucius Q.C. Lamar of Mississippi and John Tyler Morgan of Alabama. Blaine gained the respect and support of both men, although his relationship with the Alabama senator was more sustained and, despite Morgan's blatant racism, blossomed into a cordial friendship. The more courtly Senator Lamar was a conciliatory racial moderate who supported black suffrage and promoted racial accommodation in the South. In 1879, when he was still a member of the Senate, Blaine had organized a forum for the *North American Review* in which a number of prominent leaders were asked to respond to a pair of questions: "Ought the Negro to be Disfranchised? Ought He to Have Been Enfranchised?" Among those invited to participate were Senator Lamar and the future president Garfield. Blaine and Garfield, longtime advocates of black suffrage, answered "no" to the first query and "yes" to the second, as did Lamar. Blaine was pleasantly surprised at this outcome and favorably impressed with the tolerant and optimistic tone of the Mississippian's reasoned reply to the questions.

What also struck Blaine about Lamar's essay was the clear, patriotic vision of national destiny it expressed. As he noted in his concluding remarks to the forum, Senator Lamar may still have been "shackled with the narrowing dogma of State rights, and yet withal has boundless hopes for an imperial republic whose power shall lead and direct the civilization of the world." At last, thought Blaine, here was a former Confederate leader and "rebel brigadier" in Congress with whom he could work to fulfill a mutually shared vision of an imperial republic. In hopes of bringing this right-thinking gentleman on board, at least in support of the administration's foreign policy if not in allegiance to the Republican party, Blaine outlined his hemispheric blueprints to Senator Lamar just prior to assuming his duties at the State Department.[3]

The future secretary of state first proposed to call a peace conference of all Western Hemisphere nations. Its purpose would be to allow the United States to manage, control, and possibly eliminate the constant eruptions of political discord and violence that plagued the Latin American republics. Blaine feared that the all-too-frequent internal disruptions and petty border squabbles of these nations invited European, particularly British, intervention and meddling in hemispheric matters. To avoid this danger to a projected U.S. hegemony and to prevent further European encroachments, peace was essential. But that was not all, Blaine explained: control of violent outbreaks and the maintenance of stability would allow for the improved and expanded trade relations that were central to his dream of U.S. commercial preeminence.

The other proposals the secretary-designate outlined to the Mississippi Senator were projects for a Pan-American railroad to connect all the nations of the two continents and a broad network of reciprocity treaties with Latin American countries. The "Three Americas Railway" scheme was a new addition to Blaine's plans. Originally, the idea had been championed by Hinton Rowan Helper, a former American consul to Buenos Aires, Argentina, who favored increased trade and cultural contact among the nations of the Americas. Helper's lobbying efforts succeeded in having a bill introduced in the Senate in 1880 calling for federal financial support for a railway connecting North, Central, and South America. Although that legislation failed passage, then-Senator Blaine borrowed the idea and made the intercontinental railway project one of his hemispheric priorities. Accompanying this new feature of his blueprints was what was fast becoming the boilerplate signature of his proposals—reciprocity. Reciprocity treaties were touted as a commercial expansionist panacea for both Southern and Midwestern agrarians. The most versatile feature of his proposals, reciprocity proved to be an all-purpose tactic that had greater staying power and popular appeal than most of his other blueprint features.[4]

In appealing to the mushrooming Southern interest in economic growth and development with visions of overseas commercial expansion, Blaine was following the example of one of his political idols, Henry Clay, who in the antebellum period had sought to make the United States the trade emporium of the hemisphere. After becoming secretary of state, Blaine continued that approach through his strong support of and official participation in the 1881 Atlanta Cotton Exposition. He endorsed a report for the Exposition entitled, "The Cotton Goods Trade of the World," which subsequently was published and distributed by the federal government as a special consular circular for 1881. John Tyler Morgan was one Southerner who warmly praised the report and its sponsor on the floor of the Senate. The *Atlanta Constitution* also applauded the secretary's report, outlining for its readers the vast opportunities that existed for the export of American cotton products to Latin America. The editors of the newspaper were confident that the United States could outsell the British in those markets, and they believed Blaine's program was of vital concern to the South because "the export of cotton goods has become almost indispensable to our prosperity." For all of his efforts, Secretary Blaine made few political converts in the South to the Republican party, but he did win the sustained congressional endorsement of a number of Southern Democrats for his foreign policy.[5]

Not all of his new chores as secretary of state were as easily handled. Immediately after assuming the leadership of the State Department in March 1881, Blaine had the opportunity to test the workability of his imperial blueprints in a crisis situation. Actually, two issues were festering at near-crisis level when he took office; one concerned American pork exports to Europe and the other stemmed from the War of the Pacific involving Chile, Peru, and Bolivia. As frequently happens in the transition from drawing board to construction site, glitches appear that require modifications in the original plans. Henry Kissinger, a prominent secretary of state of the late twentieth century, in speaking of the challenge of managing the nation's diplomacy contended that the "convictions that leaders have formed before reaching high office are the intellectual capital they will consume as long as they continue in office." Blaine the theorist came to the State Department with more than the requisite "intellectual capital" to draw upon as he overcame his lack of experience in the day-to-day operation of foreign policy. To the unsophisticated observer, his on-the-job training might have appeared impulsive and frenetic, but Blaine never lost sight of the main prize, the glorious national destiny that was implicit in his blueprints for American empire.[6]

The agency that Blaine took over in 1881 was puny in size compared to the behemoth bureaucracy of today's State Department. The small professional staff that handled the daily correspondence barely was adequate for the growing tasks at hand. One particularly able member of the permanent staff was Alvey Adee, who rose through the ranks to become second assistant secretary in 1886, a post he held for almost forty years. The revered institutional memory of the State Department, Adee carried forward the Blaine legacy of energetic diplomacy well into the twentieth century. Representing the United States abroad were twenty-five ministers, a handful of chargés d'affaires, and about three hundred consuls tending American interests in various parts of the world. On the whole, American representatives to foreign nations were not as well-trained or as skilled as the diplomatic corps of European powers. There were exceptions to this rule. Two of the United States diplomats serving abroad at the time were prestigious men of letters and distinction, James Russell Lowell in London and Andrew D. White in Berlin. Blaine recognized the shortcomings of the foreign service and, before leaving office, recommended reforms to Garfield's successor, President Chester A. Arthur. These reforms gradually took hold over the next several decades, but it was not until the 1920s that the United States had a fully professional foreign service.

Perhaps a better indicator of the true nature of American global ambitions than the condition of the foreign service was the magnificent new building being constructed on the west side of the White House. Truly representative of the Gilded Age's excesses, the State, War, and Navy Building spoke volumes about the pretensions of an imperial republic. This structure, now the Old Executive Office Building and considered by some to be the "finest example of French Second Empire architecture in America" (although President Harry S. Truman once called it "the greatest monstrosity in America"), opened in stages beginning in 1875 when the State Department moved into the south wing. When completed in 1888, it housed three of the most important agencies fostering American overseas expansion and was believed to be the largest and most elegant office building in the world. Its floor space covers ten acres and the structure contains more than a mile and one-half of corridors that are twelve feet wide and paved in black slate and marble. In the south wing, which had been designed for the exclusive use of the State Department, the secretary's office occupied the center area of the second floor, with three windows on the south portico providing a view of the Potomac River. Adjoining the secretary's office was an elegant sixty-foot reception room designed to awe and impress visiting foreign diplomats and dignitaries.

This monumental Victorian masterpiece was imperial architecture at its grandest, signaling to the world that Washington was preparing to be the next seat of global power. A decade after its official opening, the building's symbolic tie to America's imperial ambitions became

ARTIST'S DRAWING OF THE STATE, WAR AND NAVY BUILDING

Reproduced from Harper's Weekly - April 20, 1872

Artist's Drawing of the State, War, and Navy Department (1872). Courtesy of the Old Executive Office Building.

manifestly apparent when two bronze cannons were placed, and remain to this day, at the Pennsylvania Avenue entrance. These cannons had been captured from the Spanish in 1898 during the Spanish-American War, the nation's first war for overseas empire. A century later in the 1990s, the nation's imperial success was candidly and matter-of-factly acknowledged in a descriptive visitors' brochure containing this message from President Bill Clinton: "The old saying, 'if only these walls could talk,' fits this building most appropriately. It was here in the Old State, War and Navy Building, which is now the OEOB, that America's role as a world super power was born."[7]

Given these splendid and extravagant surroundings, Secretary Blaine undoubtedly enjoyed going to his office to conduct the nation's diplomacy. However, at times the sublime quickly gave way to the mundane, if not the ridiculous. Waiting on his desk when he first arrived were summaries of recent European actions restricting the importation of American pork products. In the forefront of this effort to ban American pork were France, Germany, and Great Britain. The Europeans claimed it was an issue of public health; they were reacting to reports that American pork was diseased and, when consumed, caused painful, horrible deaths. The main source for this alarm was a sensational report by George Crump, British vice consul in Philadelphia, which was printed in British newspapers and quickly spread to the press of the continent. Crump's description of a farmer dying of trichinosis poisoning after eating pork sausages resembled a scene from a late twentieth-century blood-and-gore horror film. A doctor discovered trichinae in the victim, Crump said, and "worms were in his flesh by the millions, being scraped and squeezed from the pores of the skin. They are felt creeping through his flesh, and are literally eating up his substance."[8]

Secretary Blaine immediately denounced Crump's story as a total fabrication. He defended the purity and healthfulness of American pork products and sent stern notes to the French government, which had imposed restrictions just prior to Blaine's takeover of the State Department. The secretary also supplied the American minister to France with information about the wholesomeness of the American livestock industry and testimonials attesting to the sanitary conditions in the nation's meatpacking plants. Protecting the integrity of American pork was serious, if uninspiring, business because pork products were an important component of the export boom that restored prosperity and lifted the United States out of the depression of the 1870s. At one point in his diplomatic remonstrances, Blaine even raised the possibility of retaliation against French wines unless the restrictions were suspended. Blaine's efforts failed in the short run, although a few years later—after he had left the State Department—the French acquiesced to the pressure and allowed American pork free entry into their country. But even without a clear-cut diplomatic victory for the American hog during his nine-month tenure as secretary, Blaine had won the gratitude of the nation's farmers and agricultural businessmen for doing battle on their behalf.

The other crisis that greeted Secretary Blaine when he took office in March 1881 was the War of the Pacific. This conflict, which erupted in 1879, pitted Chile against Bolivia and Peru for control of contested Pacific Coast territory that was rich in guano (the dried dung of seabirds or bats) and nitrate, both much-coveted agricultural fertilizers in the late nineteenth century. Chile had been victorious on the battlefield in the first year of the war and appeared intent on exacting a total surrender from its defeated foes, especially Peru. Bolivia had accepted its loss and essentially became a nonplayer in the dispute. Before leaving office, William M. Evarts, Blaine's predecessor at the State Department, unsuccessfully attempted to mediate a peace accord. Blaine chose a similar, if not quite identical, approach. He first instructed his newly appointed ministers to the two warring nations to offer the good offices of the United States to bring the belligerents to the peace table. However, he stipulated that any settlement had to leave Peru intact as a nation. When that stipulation, laudable in the abstract, became apparent to the Chileans, they suspected the new American initiative was tainted with a pro-Peruvian bias. Chile refused to accept the United States as an honest broker and not only did peace remain elusive but American-Chilean relations soured as a consequence.

To be sure, not all of the responsibility for this initial failure was attributable to Blaine's instructions. The two ministers he sent proved to be incompetent bunglers, each breaking a cardinal rule of diplomacy by identifying too closely with the interests of the country in which they served. In early December 1881, to salvage his discredited peace initiative, Blaine sent a new delegation to Peru and Chile: William Trescott, a veteran diplomat, and his son Walker Blaine, who had been serving as third assistant secretary of state. Secretary Blaine appointed the Trescott mission when he knew his days at the State Department were numbered. President Garfield had been mortally wounded by an assassin in July, just a few months after his inauguration. When Garfield died on September 19, Blaine realized that the new president, Chester A. Arthur, would quickly replace him as secretary of state. Consequently, the new mission to Peru and Chile seemed an act of desperation, albeit one with an ambitious agenda. Among other things, Minister Trescott was instructed to invite the belligerents to resolve their dispute at a Pan-American conference to be held in Washington the following year. Earlier, Secretary Blaine, with President Arthur's sanction, had issued separate invitations to the proposed conference to most of the other nations of Latin America.[9]

Within a month after Blaine's resignation as secretary of state, his successor Frederick Frelinghuysen had sabotaged the Plumed Knight's Latin American diplomacy. Frelinghuysen, who along with Arthur was a member of a rival Republican party faction that despised James G. Blaine, ended the Trescott mediation initiative and rescinded the invitations to a hemispheric conference. Then in early January 1882 the Arthur administration, in a blatant maneuver to discredit Blaine's Latin American policy, sent the entire confidential correspondence surrounding the Chile-Peru imbroglio to Congress; it subsequently was made public after being leaked to the press. The Chilean minister in Washington immediately telegraphed the information about Frelinghuysen's new instructions to Santiago, while the new secretary mailed the dispatch to Trescott by sea via Panama. (It was the nineteenth-century equivalent of e-mail versus snail mail.) When the American presented his credentials in Santiago, the Chilean foreign minister knew of Frelinghuysen's revised instructions. Trescott did not and was cruelly humiliated. The coup de grâce came in April 1882 when President Arthur officially withdrew the invitations to the Pan-American conference. Blaine's hemispheric diplomacy lay in shambles.

James G. Blaine fared no better on the home scene. After the Arthur administration published his diplomatic correspondence, Blaine was vilified by his political enemies and called to account by a host of journalists and editors. He was denounced as a bellicose meddler and corrupt practitioner of "guano diplomacy," who sought to make a financial killing by supporting the specious claims of unscrupulous entrepreneurs and hustlers to guano deposits in Peru. The charges led to a House Foreign Affairs Committee investigation into the propriety of the actions of Blaine's ministers to Peru and Chile to determine whether they were "personally interested in or improperly connected with business transactions in which the intervention of this government was requested or expected." Further, the committee was instructed to inquire into allegations "that certain papers in relation to the same subjects have been improperly lost or removed from the files of the State department." The committee's investigation, which ran from March through August 1882, included public hearings and testimony by invited witnesses and government officials, including Blaine himself.[10]

The former secretary of state denied the allegations and ably defended himself in the press and in his appearance before the committee, although at one point during his personal testimony he apparently lost his temper during aggressive questioning from Perry Belmont, a thirty-year-old Democrat from New York who was serving his first term in the House. In an explosive exchange between the veteran public servant and the novice congressman, Blaine charged that his antagonist was simply a tool of "the dirty Democratic press throughout the United States." Young Belmont angrily replied in kind, calling Blaine "a bully and a coward." This highly charged personal confrontation was grist for the mill of the rabidly partisan media; Blaine was cast as either villain or hero, depending on the political identity of the newspaper or journal. Ultimately, the Plumed Knight was totally exonerated of all charges of wrongdoing in the committee's final report. Whether or not the charges of improper behavior and diplomatic blunders hurt his future presidential aspirations is debatable, but Blaine probably was correct in assuming that that was the goal of his enemies on both sides of the aisle in Congress.[11]

Beyond defending himself against the narrow charges of corruption and guano diplomacy, Blaine justified his aggressive handling of the Peruvian-Chilean conflict as necessary to counteract British meddling in the War of the Pacific. In an interview with a reporter in January 1882, the former secretary of state charged that Chile successfully humbled Peru because Great Britain supplied the victor with the necessary money, material, and muskets. When asked by the reporter if that meant he believed Britain had instigated the war, Blaine replied "to blame England would be childish." But his ambivalence surfaced and he was neither able to contain his jealousy nor to keep his anti-British feelings in check. While he admired Great Britain's growing commercial success and power, Blaine did not wish it exercised at his nation's expense. He especially did not like "to see England winning great commercial triumphs in a field that legitimately belongs to the United States, and which the United States could readily command if she would." Chile's victory had demonstrated just how quickly American commercial interests could be wiped out on South America's Pacific coast. Blaine's well-conceived Latin American program was designed to prevent further erosion of American influence and ultimately overcome Great Britain's commercial predominance in the region.[12]

In that context several points should be clarified about Blaine's

Latin American policy during the Garfield administration. First, it was not without precedent. Second, it was a collaborative effort between president and secretary of state, although after Garfield's assassination the policy became solely Blaine's handiwork. Third, it was not an impromptu endeavor. In formulating their program of Pan-Americanism, both men drew upon intellectual capital acquired during their congressional careers. Just fifteen years earlier, when Blaine and Garfield were up-and-coming members of the House, another Pacific war caught their attention. In 1866, in the last-ditch phase of a vainglorious and doomed campaign to recreate a South American empire, Spain was engaged in a naval conflict with Chile, Peru, Bolivia, and Ecuador. This war set off alarm bells among Republicans who were intent upon enforcing the Monroe Doctrine by ending Europe's reign of influence in the hemisphere. And when the startling news of the March 31 Spanish bombardment of Valparaiso, Chile reached Washington, Representative Blaine angrily denounced it as a "barbarous" and wanton attack. He asked for unanimous consent for a resolution requesting that the president pass on to the House of Representatives any information he may have or receive on the Spanish bombardment. One member objected, which immediately killed Blaine's resolution.[13]

However, some six months later the House unanimously approved a more specific resolution that served as a clear precedent for Blaine's 1881 invitation to the states of the hemisphere to attend a Pan-American conference designed, among other matters, to resolve a war of the Pacific. The December 1866 resolution expressed concern that "wars destructive of commerce and injurious and prejudicial to republican institutions have for some time been carried on between Spain and several of the South American States on the Pacific coast" and called upon the Committee on Foreign Affairs to "inquire and report whether the friendly offices of the United States ought not to be used, if practicable, to promote peace and harmony in South America." Nothing much came of this initiative for peaceful mediation, but it did demonstrate a decided continuity of purpose within Republican ranks concerning the need to control events in Latin America and assert the United States' hegemony in the hemisphere. In addition to the 1866 resolution there was another Civil War–era precedent for the GOP's Pan-Americanism. In developing their policies, Blaine and Garfield also were following the advice offered by their House colleague, Henry Winter Davis, who in 1864 urged the United States "to lead the sisterhood of American republics in the paths of peace, prosperity, and power."[14]

Blaine knew his spirited Latin American diplomacy and his challenge to British economic supremacy in the hemisphere would be popular in those Midwestern states that were the "heart" of the Republican party. After all, he and Garfield had consciously tailored their foreign policy with that constituency in mind. But their policy, as hoped, also found surprising favor with some Southern Democrats, one of whom, Representative Washington C. Whitthorne of Tennessee, lavishly praised the policy on the floor of the House in March 1882. Whitthorne, who shared Blaine's vision of American progress and grandeur, wanted a vigorous foreign policy and patriotic statesmen to guide the nation's destiny. He lauded the Garfield administration as one dedicated to overcoming sectionalism by emphasizing economic issues that held broad appeal and cut across sectional lines. "Full many a patriot of both parties," Whitthorne believed, "was more than anxious that the bitterness of sectional strife should cease." Apparently forgiving the partisan Republican Blaine for his past inflammatory waving of the "bloody shirt" and his blocking of restored citizenship rights for Confederate President Jefferson Davis, the Tennesseean applauded Blaine's Latin American policy and endorsed the call for a future Pan-American conference. Then, in a flattering comparison that must have been gratifying to the beleaguered former secretary of state, Whitthorne concluded: "Sir, let it be said to the honor of the late administration that it seems in its foreign policy to have been imbued with the teachings of the grand old patriots, whose words and deeds illustrated with brilliant luster the brightest, bravest pages of American history."[15]

One specific action taken during the Garfield presidency that received Democratic Congressman Whitthorne's hearty approval as well as enthusiastic endorsements from the Republican rank and file was Blaine's attempt to modify or terminate the Clayton-Bulwer Treaty, the 1850 agreement between the United States and Great Britain. As an editor of one of Maine's leading newspapers in the late 1850s, young James G. Blaine had monitored the Anglo-American dispute surrounding implementation of the treaty. As a budding American patriot, he had resented Prime Minister Palmerston's cavalier dismissal of the United States' claims that British expansionist activities in Central America almost immediately after the treaty was signed violated the terms of the agreement. Although Lord Palmerston had acquiesced to the American interpretation of the treaty and President Buchanan subsequently had dropped his threat to abrogate the Clayton-Bulwer agreement, Blaine learned a valuable lesson: power was what counted in international relations. In the early 1880s a new power relationship existed. The United States was rapidly becoming the nation to be reckoned with in the Western Hemisphere and, as secretary of state, Blaine intended to drive this point home to his British counterparts. Premature in his expectations about American power and prestige, Blaine brashly overplayed his hand. It would take another two decades before Great Britain totally acquiesced to American demands to properly modify and effectively terminate the Clayton-Bulwer Treaty.

Blaine's bold Central American canal policy was driven by a sense of urgency. In late December 1879 Ferdinand de Lesseps, the flamboyant French entrepreneur and triumphant builder of the Suez Canal, appeared in Panama to begin work on an interoceanic canal. Many Americans were shocked at de Lesseps' audacity because they had assumed such a project was strictly within their nation's domain. It was the swiftness with which the French enterprise had been launched—a matter of months—that particularly alarmed Congress and the Hayes administration. After the government and the public recovered from their surprise, the majority expressed the preference for an exclusively "American" canal. Both the Congress and the President acted immediately to protect and guarantee the United States' vital and special interest in an isthmian waterway. House and Senate resolutions were passed reaffirming the Monroe Doctrine and implicitly denouncing this French-led European venture. In a special message to Congress in March 1880, President Hayes made clear, as Ulysses S. Grant had before him, that "the policy of this country is a canal under American control. The United States can not consent to the surrender of this control to any European power or to any combination of European powers." Hayes justified his claim to American primacy in the isthmian region on the premise that a completed waterway would be an extension of the American coastline linking the nation's Atlantic and Pacific shores.[16]

Congress escalated the rhetorical campaign against European meddling on America's turf with an attack on the Clayton-Bulwer Treaty, thus bringing Great Britain back into the canal equation. Defining the 1850 agreement, with its stipulation for joint Anglo-American participation in any future canal project, as the main obstacle to an exclusively American-constructed interoceanic canal, the House of Representatives passed a resolution demanding the abrogation of the Clayton-Bulwer Treaty. The Hayes administration balked at this recommendation, declining to abrogate unilaterally an international treaty obligation. When James G. Blaine entered the State Department in 1881 he carried forward the policy articulated by President Hayes and implicit in his own blueprints for American empire. In June he wrote the American minister to Great Britain, James Russell Lowell, detailing the Garfield administration's general position on an isthmian waterway and the United States' specific opposition to the attempts by the great powers of Europe to guarantee the neutrality of the projected de Lesseps canal across the Isthmus of Panama. Secretary Blaine reasserted the Hayes argument that a canal would be part of the American coastline and took the logic one step further. Because of the tremendous growth of the Pacific slope states, which "are imperial in extent," any future interoceanic canal would "be as truly a channel of communication between the Eastern and Western States as our own transcontinental railways." Nowhere in this discourse on an isthmian canal did Blaine mention the Clayton-Bulwer Treaty.[17]

Not surprisingly, when the British foreign secretary, Lord Granville, got around to answering the American secretary five months later, he rejected Blaine's ingenious logic and politely referred him to the Clayton-Bulwer Treaty. In November an impatient Blaine, only just beginning to recover from the trauma of Garfield's death, sent a second dispatch to Lowell before receiving Granville's reply to his first note. On this occasion, without prior prompting by the British government, Blaine did discuss and seek revision of the Clayton-Bulwer agreement. Modification of the treaty was required and justified, Secretary Blaine argued, because the United States "will not consent to perpetuate any treaty that impeaches our rightful and long-established claim to priority on the American continent." American hegemony in the Western Hemisphere demanded that every "part of the treaty which forbids the United States to fortify the canal and hold political control of it in conjunction with the country in which it is located, to be canceled." The issue of the neutrality of a future canal was "an American question" to be dealt with "by the American powers." Blaine was unequivocally stating, and attempting to fulfill Monroe's legacy, that in future international power configurations, the Americas were to be for Americans.[18]

After receiving Lord Granville's reply to his first dispatch to Lowell, which had ignored specific treatment of the Clayton-Bulwer Treaty, Blaine sent a third and last message on the subject to his minister in London. The lame-duck secretary of state now donned his historian's hat. Using the printed and unprinted diplomatic correspondence from the period to detail the United States' historical objections to the agreement, Blaine also drew upon his own firsthand experience as a journalist in the 1850s who had covered the controversial issues surrounding the treaty's implementation in Central America. What struck him as a historian analyzing the three-decade-old treaty was its "elastic character." More conciliatory on this occasion, Secretary Blaine optimistically forecast that with British acceptance of the modifications concerning fortification and political control suggested in his second dispatch, a revised Clayton-Bulwer Treaty would serve as "a full and perfect settlement for all time" on Central America.[19]

When this private diplomatic correspondence on the interoceanic canal became public, Blaine's message was clear to the foreign as well as the domestic audience. His friend and sometime confidante, Andrew Carnegie, provided a particularly revealing commentary that spanned both poles of the Anglo-American connection. Carnegie, who had arrived in his adopted country a penniless immigrant from Scotland and had become a fabulously wealthy capitalist who seemed the epitome of the American Dream, told Blaine he was "exactly right" about the treaty, proclaiming that "America is going to control anything & everything on this continent—that's settled." The millionaire industrialist further informed Blaine that the "highest authority" of the British print media, *The Spectator* of London, "agreed with your claim." Carnegie was correct. The editors of *The Spectator* not only accepted Blaine's argument but also believed nothing in his actions on the interoceanic canal, or for that matter in the Chile-Peru conflict, was "in the least inconsistent with European diplomacy." The United States' interest in Panama was similar to Britain's objectives in Egypt and India, or France's preoccupation with North Africa.[20]

During Secretary Blaine's brief nine-month tenure at the State Department, the Hawaiian Islands also served as a diplomatic battleground between the United States and Great Britain. Initially, Anglo-American tension grew out of the 1875 reciprocity treaty between the United States and Hawaii. British officials objected to the preferential treatment accorded to the United States by the terms of the agreement, which they claimed violated the most-favored-nation clause of Britain's own treaty with the island kingdom. Blaine's predecessors at the State Department had ignored these protests, which by 1881 led a frustrated British government to demand that the Hawaiian monarchy grant British merchants refunds on all customs duties greater than those paid by Americans since the reciprocity treaty took effect. Secretary Blaine made clear to both the Hawaiians and the British that any extension of the privileges granted in the 1875 treaty to another power would be a flagrant violation of the reciprocity agreement. In this case the American interpretation of reciprocity prevailed and the British never successfully countered the reciprocity tactic, especially as it later was extended to Latin American countries, until well into the twentieth century.

Meanwhile, King Kalakaua, who traveled to the United States in

1874–75 to lobby for the reciprocity treaty, was planning another overseas voyage, this time one that would girdle the world. Blaine and Garfield, who as members of the House of Representatives had met the king during his earlier visit, feared that the purpose of Kalakaua's newly scheduled global trip was to find a European power, possibly England or France, to buy the islands. As a congressman, Garfield had supported reciprocity, and as president, he stressed to his cabinet "the importance of the Sandwich Islands in relation to the future commerce of the Pacific and the Isthmus canal or railway." Shortly after the cabinet meeting, President Garfield confided to one of his closest friends that conditions in Hawaii "give us a good deal of anxiety. The king has started on a voyage around the world, and it is feared he is contemplating either the sale of the islands or some commercial treaty with European powers which would embarrass the United States." Secretary Blaine had come to distrust King Kalakaua as a "false and intriguing man" intent on finding a European buyer to purchase his kingdom. In discussions with both the French and English ministers, the American secretary of state informed them that Article IV of the 1875 treaty prohibited the Hawaiian monarch from selling his kingdom. The Garfield administration's anxieties proved unwarranted. King Kalakaua did not auction off the islands and remained committed to the terms of the 1875 reciprocity treaty.[21]

A more serious threat to the American position in Hawaii came from a British scheme to import large numbers of Indian laborers from the subcontinent of Asia into the islands as a source of cheap labor. James M. Comly, the American minister to the Hawaiian Islands, relayed the information about this plan to Secretary Blaine, who in a series of responses to Minister Comly outlined his objections to the proposal. Blaine feared such a labor arrangement ultimately would subvert the independence of Hawaii by joining it to an "Asiatic system." That was unacceptable. If the islands were to "drift from their independent station it must be toward assimilation and identification with the American system, to which they belong by the operation of natural laws, and must belong by the operation of political necessity." Using the idiom of his idol and mentor Henry Clay to define the limits of American commercial empire, Blaine proceeded to make one of his most comprehensive statements on the nature of what he now explicitly labeled an "American system."

Drawing upon the intellectual capital that he been accumulating and the imperial blueprints that he had been devising over the past quarter century, dating back to his tutelage by Luther Severance, the United States' first commissioner to the Sandwich Islands, Secretary

Blaine clarified Hawaii's position in the grand plan. The secretary of state began his explanation of the "American system" with a historical review of the enormous economic growth of the Pacific states and their importance to the future development of the Union. The purchase of Alaska in 1867 by another of Blaine's mentors, Secretary of State William H. Seward, had further enhanced and enriched the nation's Pacific domain. The limits of the United States' west coast commercial domain would be marked by San Francisco at the center, then "a line drawn northwestwardly to the Aleutian group, marks our Pacific border almost to the confines of Asia. A corresponding line drawn southwestwardly from San Francisco to Honolulu marks the natural limit of the ocean belt within which our trade with the oriental countries must flow." Blaine then tied his Panama canal policy to Hawaii with the argument that "the extension of commercial empire westward from those states is no less vitally important to their development than is their communication with the Eastern coast by the Isthmian channel." The strategic control possessed by the Hawaiian Islands over the North Pacific "brings their possession within the range of purely American policy, as much as that of the Isthmus itself." There was no doubt that America was to have a Pacific empire; Hawaii and the Panama Canal were crucial to the realization of that vision. (To understand his vision see the accompanying map of the Pacific Rim).

But Secretary Blaine went still further in explaining his blueprints for creating an American commercial empire to rival and surpass that of Great Britain. In so doing, the Republican leader foreshadowed the American informal empire that was to become a reality in the twentieth century under the direction, at least initially, of one of his star pupils, future Secretary of State John Hay. First, Blaine asserted that the nation's Pacific and Atlantic policies were complementary. Although the Atlantic at that time was considered an English lake, Blaine foresaw the day when the Gulf of Mexico would be the door, with Cuba as the key, to American hegemony in the Western Hemisphere. The analogy Blaine constructed was as follows: "Hawaii, although much farther from the Californian coast than is Cuba from the Floridian peninsula, holds in the western sea much the same position as Cuba in the Atlantic. It is the key to the maritime dominion of the Pacific states, as Cuba is to the Gulf trade." In these dispatches to Minister Comly, which he eventually discussed as well with the British minister to the United States, Blaine disavowed any intention on the part of his government to annex either Hawaii or Cuba, although in his imperial blueprints they were integral insular parts of his "American commercial system."[22]

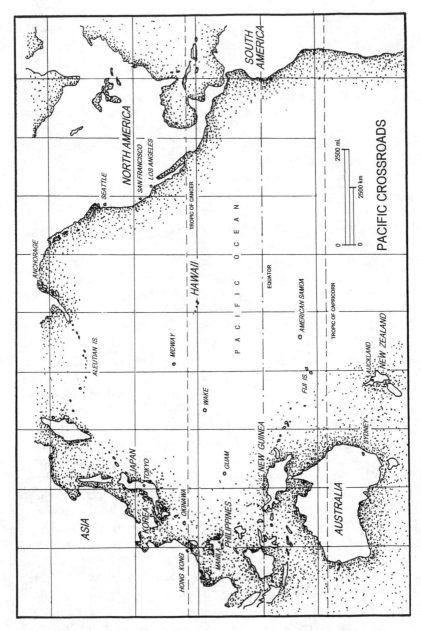

Pacific Crossroads. Map by Ed Pease.

Another phase of Blaine's ambitious project for a Pacific Rim commercial system involved the hermit kingdom of Korea. During his nine months at the helm of the State Department, Blaine set in motion the events that led to the United States' first treaty with that nation. Previous attempts to open Korea to American influence and commerce had all been rebuffed. The most recent unsuccessful overture had been made in 1880 by Commodore Robert W. Shufeldt, an American naval officer and tireless promoter of American commercial expansion in the Pacific. No sooner had Blaine become secretary of state than Shufeldt was at his office door urging him to endorse another mission to secure a Korean treaty. What Shufeldt proposed was that he be sent to China as a naval attaché, ostensibly to advise the Chinese in their efforts to modernize their navy but secretly assigned to negotiate a treaty with Korea under Chinese auspices. The plan appealed to the new secretary's sense of intrigue and adventure. Less than two weeks after he assumed the reins at State, Blaine appointed Shufeldt as his executive agent entrusted with a commission to negotiate what would be Korea's first treaty with a western power. Initially, Shufeldt made little progress in breaking down Korean resistance to pursuing any diplomatic agreement with the United States, but he ultimately succeeded in negotiating a treaty of amity and commerce in 1882 that opened Korea to American merchants, missionaries, and diplomats.

Blaine's aggressive handling of the nation's diplomacy during his nine months in office as secretary of state had established him in the minds of thousands of his countrymen as "the first American Statesman of the present day." His capacity for hard work was well known to those who served with him in Congress, but his energy and drive astonished his State Department subordinates. Without previous diplomatic experience or service in the executive branch, Blaine proved up to the task. Years later one of his still-awed staff remarked that his thorough knowledge and understanding of foreign affairs "was a marvel not only to his friends in Washington, but to the Foreign Ministers and trained diplomatists, residing in the Capital City." Secretary Blaine did attempt to accomplish a great deal in a short period of time, and it must be acknowledged that, in the final analysis, his expansionist reach far exceeded his imperial grasp.[23]

Of course, that failure to achieve concrete results might be explained by the fact that President Garfield was assassinated, which led to Blaine's removal from office. But some unanswered questions remain about Blaine's actions after President Garfield died in September 1881. Although he was devastated by his friend's death, Blaine stayed on as secretary of state for another three months and much of what he did—extending invitations to a Pan-American conference, sending strong notes to his ministers about the American position on the isthmian canal and Hawaii, and updating Shufeldt's instructions for a Korean treaty—came at the eleventh hour. Why did he send out a battery of his most important correspondence in November and December 1881 when he knew he was a lame duck and his successor was awkwardly waiting in the wings for Blaine to leave the stage? Skeptics and critics have maintained to the present day that these last-minute diplomatic acrobatics unquestionably were calculated to win public support and make him the logical candidate for the Republican nomination in the next presidential election.

Perhaps the critics are correct. But another supplementary interpretation, not totally at odds with their explanation, adds to our understanding of Blaine's motivations and actions. Over the years as journalist and legislator, the Maine Republican had devised a foreign policy plan and the detailed blueprints for its implementation. Not even the pain of Garfield's death and the loss of a kindred spirit in the White House would prevent James G. Blaine from placing his program before the American public and the world at large. It was not a reckless or irrational course of action. Blaine reasoned that his successor as secretary of state would have no choice but to finish what he had initiated, especially if the proposals had President Arthur's prior approval. At first, it appeared that Blaine had badly miscalculated and his scheme had backfired. Frelinghuysen, also with Arthur's blessing, staged a partisan assault to discredit Blaine's foreign policy by making his diplomatic correspondence public and retracting the invitations to the Pan-American conference. Consequently, Blaine was pilloried in the press and publicly ridiculed as "Jingo Jim," a description that pejoratively cast him as a belligerent, reckless, chauvinist patriot.

However, in the end Blaine was basically correct in his instincts that intraparty divisions did not override a Republican consensus on the necessity of overseas economic expansion. After initially having censored his diplomacy, Arthur and Freylinghuysen eventually came to accept Blaine's initiatives on the isthmian canal and Korea and moved, without success, to implement a program of reciprocity treaties with Latin American countries. Although they did not revive the call for a meeting of all the nations of the hemisphere, the idea had caught on, remained alive in Congress, and in 1889, when Blaine returned as secretary of state in the Benjamin Harrison administration, the first Pan-American conference assembled in Washington. Before leaving office in 1885, Frelinghuysen also sustained Blaine's Hawaiian policy by beginning negotiations for a renewal of the 1875 reciprocity treaty. In some instances the Arthur administration's diplomacy even went beyond what Blaine had advocated. They negotiated a treaty, which the Senate did not ratify, granting the United States a protectorate over Nicaragua and sent an American delegation to an international conference on the Congo. Blaine opposed these actions, being particularly critical of the venture into Africa because he feared that taking part in conferences dealing with the internal affairs of other continents invited European interference in the Western Hemisphere, which in turn might jeopardize the Monroe Doctrine.

Despite the attacks on his integrity and his diplomacy after he resigned in December 1881, Blaine was proud of his accomplishments. His blueprints for empire had been tested and modified—he now apparently favored the acquisition of Cuba, a policy he had opposed a decade earlier—and in revised form they remained the bedrock of his imperial designs. In his closing testimony to the congressional investigating committee, Blaine stated that, of any chapter of his long public life, he was most proud of the South American policy laid down by the Garfield administration. In a full-scale defense of his Latin American program that was published in September 1882, Blaine remained adamant in his conviction that the United States must assert its trade dominance in the hemisphere, for "if the commercial empire that legitimately belongs to us is to be ours, we must not lie idle and witness its transfer to others." By acting consistently on his motto of doing the bold thing at the right time, James G. Blaine had blended his foreign policy agenda with his unabated desire to someday occupy the White House.[24]

Notes

1. Quoted in Alan Peskin, "Blaine, Garfield and Latin America: A New Look," *Americas* 36 (1979):87.

2. James G. Blaine to James A. Garfield, February 16, 1881, in Gail Hamilton, *Biography of James G. Blaine* (Norwich, CT: Henry Bill Publishing Company, 1895), 502; *Milwaukee Sentinel*, November 6, 1891. Sir Lionel Sackville-West to Lord Granville, December 28, 1881, in *Private Letters from the British Embassy in Washington to the Foreign Secretary Lord Granville, 1880–1885*, eds. Paul Knaplund and Carolyn M. Clewes, Annual Report of the American Historical Association. 1941 (Washington, DC: Government Printing Office, 1942), 1:161.

3. "Ought the Negro to be Disfranchised? Ought He to Have Been Enfranchised?" *North American Review* (March 1879): 225–83.

4. Theron C. Crawford, *James G. Blaine: A Study of His Life and Career* (Philadelphia: Edgewood Publishing Company, 1893), 490–91.

5. Remarks of John Tyler Morgan, October 17, 1881, *Congressional Record*,

47th Cong., Special sess. Senate (Washington, DC: Government Printing Office, 1881), 524; *Atlanta Constitution,* February 25, 1882.

6. Quoted in Michael H. Hunt, *Ideology and U.S. Foreign Policy* (New Haven: Yale University Press, 1987), 1.

7. Jim O'Connell, "A Building by Any Other Name than the OEOB," *Washington Post,* August 10, 1997; *The Old Executive Office Building* (Washington, DC: Executive Office of the President, Office of Administration, 1993).

8. *Foreign Relations of the United States, 1881* (Washington, DC: Government Printing Office, 1882), 580.

9. David M. Pletcher, *The Awkward Years: American Foreign Relations Under Garfield and Arthur* (Columbia: University of Missouri Press, 1962), 76–79.

10. House Report, 47th Cong., 1st sess., no. 1790, 1.

11. Ibid., 238–39.

12. *New York Tribune,* January 30, 1882.

13. Remarks of James G. Blaine, May 2, 1866, *Congressional Globe,* 39th Cong., 1st sess. (Washington, DC: 1866), 2341.

14. Ibid.; resolution of John A. Bingham, December 17, 1866, 39th Cong., 2d sess., 152; remarks of Henry Winter Davis, April 4, 1864, 38th Cong., 1st sess., Part II, 1408.

15. Remarks of Washington C. Whitthorne, March 2, 1882, *Congressional Record,* 47th Cong., 1st sess. (Washington, DC: Government Printing Office, 1882), 1553–56.

16. James D. Richardson, *Messages and Papers of the Presidents,* 11 vols. (Washington, DC: Bureau of National Literature and Art, 1905), 7:585.

17. James G. Blaine, *Political Discussions: Legislative, Diplomatic and Popular* (Norwich, CT: Henry Bill Publishing Company, 1887), 311–16.

18. Ibid., 318–25.

19. Ibid., 326–35.

20. Quoted in Edward P. Crapol, *America for Americans: Economic Nationalism and Anglophobia in the Late Nineteenth Century,* (Westport, CT: Greenwood Press, 1973), 79.

21. Theodore Clarke Smith, *The Life and Letters of James A. Garfield,* 2 vols. (New Haven: Yale University Press, 1925), 2:1167; Ralph S. Kuykendall, *The Hawaiian Kingdom, Volume III, 1874–1893, The Kalakaua Dynasty* (Honolulu, University of Hawaii Press, 1967), 238–39.

22. Blaine, *Political Discussions,* 388–96.

23. Henry O'Connor, "Blaine's Nine Months as Secretary of State," 1888, Henry O'Connor Papers, Archives, Hesburgh Library, Notre Dame University, South Bend, Indiana.

24. Blaine quote reflecting on "only one chapter in my life" cited in David S. Muzzey, *James G. Blaine: A Political Idol of Other Days* (New York: Dodd, Mead and Company, 1935), 251; Sir Lionel Sackville-West to Lord Granville, no. 355, confidential, vol. 681, (London: Public Record Office); James G. Blaine, "The South American Policy of the Garfield Administration," *Chicago Weekly Magazine,* September 16, 1882, 1–3.

5

Mr. Republican, 1882–1888

Our foreign policy should be an American policy in its broadest and most comprehensive sense—a policy of peace, of friendship, of commercial enlargement.

—James G. Blaine, 1884

In 1882 James G. Blaine was out of public office for the first time in almost a quarter of a century. Still in the prime of his life—he was but fifty-two years old—this inveterate campaigner and consummate politician, who won his first election before the Civil War and who, according to Ohio Republican Senator John Sherman, "ate, drank, and breathed politics," was now in the unaccustomed position of being a private citizen. Garfield's death had been a devastating blow for Blaine. Not only had he lost a good friend and political soul mate but his dreams of greatness for the United States appeared jeopardized. Blaine rightfully had expected at least four, perhaps even eight, years as head of the State Department to implement his imperial blueprints. In anticipation of the likelihood of an extended stay in the nation's capital, the Blaines had built a grand and majestic new house at Dupont Circle that befit the pretensions of the foreign secretary of an imperial republic. But despite his lofty expectations and his sheath of blueprints for empire, cruel fate intervened to dash, at least momentarily, Blaine's high hopes for the nation's destiny.

Even though he had suffered the ignominy of public rebuke and unceremonious dismissal from office, Blaine never seriously entertained the prospect of withdrawing from the public arena into the comfortable and quiet life of an elder statesman. To be sure, he initially retreated to his family to regroup emotionally and plan a program of political damage control. However, as Mrs. Blaine wisely advised her children, there was no need to fret over this regrettable turn of events. Their resilient father would recover from this humiliating setback, and his future success was assured. In the meantime, the head of the Blaine household focused on several immediate tasks, such as retrieving his personal fortunes, preparing the Garfield eulogy he was to deliver February 1882, and tending to his railroad stock. Along with these consoling words, Mrs. Blaine also warned the children to be prepared for continued vicious personal attacks on their father's conduct while secretary of state. "Father will be vindicated in every particular," she assured her family. "His policy is a patriotic one, and the people are going to so recognize it. Not a selfish thought is in it, but it is in all its ramifications, American."[1]

Predictably, damage control became Blaine's first order of business, and he quickly went on the offensive in defending his handling of the nation's foreign policy. When Frederick Frelinghuysen, the new secretary of state, announced the withdrawal of the invitations to a Pan-American conference, Blaine wrote an open letter to President Arthur, which received national circulation after first being published in the *New York Tribune*. The former secretary of state pointedly questioned his successor's rationale for withdrawing the invitations, which was that the holding of such a conference might offend the European powers. "This is certainly a new position for the United States to assume," Blaine informed President Arthur, "and one which I earnestly beg you will not permit this Government to occupy." What troubled Blaine even more than the administration's toadying to the European powers, was that Frelinghuysen and Arthur were passing up a chance to improve the United States' trade relations with its neighbors. He described the relations as "unsatisfactory to us, and even deplorable." Blaine reminded Arthur that the projected conference originally had presidential approval and reiterated that it was designed to seek peace in the hemisphere and establish closer ties between the United States and the nations of Latin America. For Blaine, it was an article of faith that peace and stability in the hemisphere would, in turn, bring better commercial relations and expand markets for American exports and thus end the United States' unfavorable trade balance with the countries of Latin America.[2]

Blaine's carefully calculated program of damage control culminated in the late summer of 1882 with the publication of a tightly-argued explication of the Garfield administration's South American policy. This essay, which first appeared in the *Chicago Weekly Magazine*, was more than a justification and defense of past policy. It also was the lead-off effort in Blaine's renewed campaign to win converts to his, and the martyred James A. Garfield's, vision of Pan-Americanism. The main outlines of his imperial blueprints for the hemisphere were consistent and familiar, but there was a new feature in the design. In addition to the repetitive theme that peace in the hemisphere would cultivate commerce and "lead to a large increase in the export trade of the United States," the former secretary of state placed added emphasis on the role of the Monroe Doctrine in Latin America. Blaine urged a fundamental change in President James Monroe's original 1823 declaration. He proposed to elevate it from a simple warning to European nations to stay out of the hemisphere to a policy of "friendly" diplomatic interventions to restore peace and amity among feuding Latin American nations. Such well-meaning, nonmilitary interventions, Blaine assured his readers, "fall within the line of both duty and interest on the part of the United States."

Blaine's argument for modifying and modernizing the Monroe Doctrine was embedded in the logic and rationale of imperial rivalry. If the United States failed to pursue friendly, diplomatic interventions in Central and South America, the Europeans would, of necessity, fill the resulting power vacuum. It was the humane mission of the great republic of the North to intervene, because Latin American nations "require external pressure to keep them from war," and the proposed peace congress "would have raised the standard of their civilization." "Our own government," Blaine asserted, "cannot take the ground that it will not offer friendly intervention to settle troubles between American countries, unless at the same time it freely concedes to European Governments the right of such intervention, and thus consents to a practical destruction of the Monroe doctrine and an unlimited increase of European and Monarchial influence on this continent." The dynamics of imperial rivalry in the hemisphere, unleashed by a "if we don't, they will" mentality, left the United States little choice but to "perform the duty of humane intervention" and to accept the "responsibility of the great trust" that was an inherent obligation of imperial power. For Blaine, duty and trust were basic features of Anglo-Saxon mission, and integral to an imperial creed that poet Rudyard Kipling later immortalized as the "white man's burden."[3]

At the same time that Blaine was defending, as well as proselytizing for, the Garfield administration's foreign policy, he was weighing his career options. Despite his disappointment and bitterness at being removed from office and becoming the whipping boy of his political enemies, Blaine remained optimistic that at some point he would have the opportunity to reenter public life. As one concession to the elder statesman role, he began writing a history of Congress in the Republican party era, from the days of Lincoln to the death of Garfield. However, around the Blaine family dining room table the hot topic of discussion, from Christmas Day 1881 until well into the year 1882, was the question of father's future course of action. Perhaps as an instinctive defense mechanism, Mrs. Blaine ruled out another try for the White House for her husband. Apparently, Blaine agreed, deciding that the State Department was the best alternative. "He says there is only one position which he craves in the future," Harriet Blaine reported to family members who were temporarily away from the homestead, "the Presidency may go, but he would like to carry out his views of statecraft in 1885 as Secretary of State."[4]

That privately expressed family preference quickly was subsumed, however, by both James G. Blaine's burning political ambition and the undeniable and simple fact that in the minds of many party leaders and in the hearts of most of the GOP rank and file, he was "Mr. Republican." Blaine richly deserved this loyalty and adulation from the party faithful. In virtually every election year since the late 1860s, he had hit the rails to make campaign swings through the states of the Northeast and Middle West in support of the Republican party and its candidates for statewide and national office. He had paid his political dues, and the imagery of "Blaine on the train" would be, in retrospect, one appropriate symbol for the political culture of the Gilded Age. The Plumed Knight rode trains and used the nation's modern railroad network in the same way that late twentieth-century political candidates rely on airliners, personal jets, and helicopters. As Mr. Republican, he routinely employed the telegraph and telephone in the same fashion that present-day politicians use television, fax machines, the Internet, and e-mail. Blaine easily converted the rapidly changing technology of his day into the handmaiden of his political ambitions. Indeed, he may have been the first modern politician, unafraid as he was to exploit every new invention to his advantage. Certainly, others learned from him. As young and up-and-coming politicians, both William McKinley and Theodore Roosevelt observed and emulated Blaine's success.

James G. Blaine proved to be a master in the use of the print media as well. Despite the technological changes that swept the nation, newspapers and magazines remained, as they had been throughout the history of the republic, the predominant and traditional source of information for most Americans. A clear and concise writer, Blaine eagerly and regularly took up his pen to explain and defend his political agenda and foreign policy blueprints to the American public. He also occasionally planted anonymous stories in the press and frequently sent suggested editorials to his good friend Whitelaw Reid, editor of the *New York Tribune*. These editorials, often as not, appeared only slightly altered in the next day's editions. An expert in the use of the late nineteenth-century's equivalent of the sound bite, Blaine effectively linked the GOP's advocacy of the protective tariff with patriotism and "true Americanism," while in the same breath stigmatizing the Democrats as un-American, pro-British free traders. "America for Americans" became the catchphrase, used by Blaine and a host of others, that appealed to and reinforced the public's visceral Anglophobia and anti-British nationalism. But Blaine's sound bites proved issue-specific, timebound, and ephemeral. His political writings did not produce a memorable, lasting epigram or aphorism, except perhaps the cryptic reminder to recipients of his correspondence to "burn this letter."

Blaine's success as Mr. Republican hinged as well on the traditional face-to-face skills of the professional politician. He loved pressing the flesh, shaking hands and mingling with the voters, most of whom were still from small towns and rural areas, to talk about the weather, crops, prices, and their personal hopes and dreams. Blaine rarely forgot a name. Years after a first meeting, he could step from a train in any number of cities and towns in America's heartland and almost instantly recognize the person, effortlessly renew a conversation on politics, and easily catch up on family and friends. By all accounts, Mr. Republican was both a hale fellow well met and a mellifluous and mesmerizing orator, at a time in the nation's history when both talents were highly prized. As Julia B. Foraker, the wife of an Ohio Republican leader, recalled in her memoir: "Who that heard him can ever forget the speech Blaine made from the balcony of the Burnet House that September night. . . . Moonlight, and Blaine's silvery voice. People were bewitched by Blaine; it was almost uncanny. The man's curious hypnotic power never lessened." According to Mrs. Foraker, "Blaine radiated glamour and warmth when he did things. Had he been a woman, people would have rushed off to send expensive flowers."[5]

Further confirmation of Blaine's unquestioned status as the nation's most popular Republican came in late February 1882. William McKinley, a rising GOP star from Ohio who shared Julia B. Foraker's appreciation of the Plumed Knight's magnetic personality, had persuaded a reluctant, grief-stricken Blaine to deliver the nation's official eulogy for the slain President Garfield. The eulogy, over which Blaine tearfully toiled for almost six weeks, was delivered in the House chamber before President Arthur and his cabinet, the Supreme Court justices, members of the House and Senate, the diplomatic corps and packed galleries of the families of government officials and the few fortunate general spectators who received tickets to the event. On that somber occasion Blaine was greeted with hearty applause, performed admirably, and did not disappoint his audience. It was not a memorable speech but an emotionally satisfying piece of romantic and heroic puffery that lamented unfulfilled promise and a life cut tragically short. As Harriet Blaine matter-of-factly reported to an absent family member, "The Eulogy was fine and tender, and concise and interesting to the last degree, was listened to with untiring interest, and has been followed by an almost unbroken stream of congratulations."[6]

After delivering the Garfield eulogy, Blaine's national fame soared, never waning during the Arthur presidency. More popular with the American people than the occupant of the White House, Mr. Republican appeared destined to be the party's nominee in 1884. Constantly in the public eye and at times portrayed unfavorably because of intense scrutiny by congressional and media critics of his alleged blundering and jingoistic foreign policy, Blaine kept his composure, all the while making sure that his imperial blueprints remained intact. For example, in early 1883 it appeared that the reciprocity treaty with Hawaii, which had been intended to tie those islands to the United States with "hoops of steel," would not be renewed. Leading the campaign against renewal was Senator Justin Morrill of Vermont, Blaine's longtime friend and traveling companion during a trip to Europe in the late 1860s. Now the powerful chairman of the Senate Finance Committee, Morrill and his fellow committee members charged that the Hawaiian reciprocity treaty was "adverse to the interests of the United States" and "nothing less than its abrogation affords a sufficient remedy." Morrill was an old-fashioned pocketbook determinist. He evaluated the benefits of reciprocity solely in narrow economic terms. For Blaine, however, reciprocity was more than a ledger-balancing exercise involving dollars and cents. It was the fulcrum in a global strategy upon which hinged future American political and commercial preeminence in the Pacific Rim.[7]

Although he was on the sidelines and without the power base of an elected or appointed national office, an alarmed Blaine began a personal lobbying campaign to save the treaty. The cajoling on behalf of reciprocity began in a letter to Senator William B. Allison, a Republican ally from Iowa. Blaine warned Allison that it would be "a horrible mistake to rescind that treaty *now*." Next, he confronted the main opponent to treaty renewal, Senator Morrill. Explaining to his venerable Republican compatriot that "I came into very close relations with the important facts behind that convention when I was Secy of State," Blaine admitted that if "you treat it simply as a revenue matter it is not defensible." But there were "other very important" strategic and diplomatic considerations that justified renewal. In 1883–84 Blaine did help stave off abrogation of the treaty. Several years later, in 1887, the Senate finally approved a renegotiated Hawaiian reciprocity treaty after the insertion of an amendment granting the United States exclusive use of Pearl Harbor as a coaling and repair station. The Pearl Harbor proviso was the handiwork of his old friend Senator John Tyler Morgan, the Alabama Democrat, and was supported by several of Blaine's Republican expansionist allies on the Senate Foreign Relations Committee, including his protégé from Maine William P. Frye, George F. Edmunds of Vermont, former Secretary of State William M. Evarts, and future President Benjamin Harrison.[8]

In the early months of 1884, as the presidential campaign began, James G. Blaine was the consensus front-runner for the Republican nomination. By keeping himself busy managing a program of damage control to preserve his foreign policy blueprints, Blaine had contained and overcome his grief over Garfield's death, all the while basking in the public limelight. The appearance that spring of the first volume of *Twenty Years of Congress* added to his intellectual and political luster. Blaine was in position to wrest his party's nomination from an incumbent president, Chester A. Arthur. Poised to attain the ultimate goal of his political life, the mercurial Blaine entertained private doubts about seeking the presidency. As he often privately confided to Mrs. Blaine, his true "Ebenezer," or place of refuge and hope, was the Department of State, not the White House. Perhaps it was this ambivalence that prompted Blaine to write to the popular federal judge, Walter Q. Gresham, offering to support him for the GOP nomination if Gresham in return would appoint him secretary of state. Although Gresham thought this "a square proposition," he declined Blaine's deal. Unbeknownst to Blaine, Judge Gresham was his mortal political enemy who secretly had schemed to deny him the 1876 nomination with the revelation of the Mulligan letters.[9]

Another explanation for Blaine's ambivalence and uncertainty about making a run for the presidency in 1884 was the unsettling realization that, despite his vast popularity, he probably would not win election. One prominent Ohio Republican, Murat Halstead of Cincinnati, declared years later that Blaine did not want the GOP nomination in 1884 because he knew he could not win New York state and hence could not win the presidency. In an article published in *McClure's Magazine* in 1896, Halstead revealed that Blaine had sent him a telegram in the week before the national Republican convention was to meet in Chicago, asking him to come to Washington to talk over the question of the nomination. When Halstead arrived the two men discussed the upcoming convention, and Blaine blurted out, "I am alarmed." He explained to his guest that he feared he would be nominated and wanted the Ohioan's help "in preventing my nomination." Dumbfounded, Halstead asked why. Blaine replied, "The objection to my nomination is that I cannot be elected. With the South solid against us we cannot succeed without New York, and I cannot carry that State." His defeat in New York might be by "just a little," Blaine conceded, but nonetheless "it would be a mistake to nominate me." Halstead declined to block his friend's candidacy, and the Republican party at its Chicago convention nominated the apparently reluctant, although remarkably prescient, Blaine on the fourth ballot.[10]

There were a few warning signs during the convention's proceedings that justified the Plumed Knight's gloomy foreboding. Two political saplings destined for future greatness as mighty oaks in their service to party and nation, Theodore Roosevelt of New York and Henry Cabot Lodge of Massachusetts, championed the reform-minded candidate, George F. Edmunds of Vermont. Senator Edmunds was every bit as vocal and dedicated an overseas expansionist as Blaine, but the Vermonter was not identified as a Gilded Age spoilsman tainted by corruption and graft. The reformers, eagerly led by Roosevelt and Lodge, achieved an initial victory by defeating the Blaine candidate for the mostly honorary post of temporary chairman of the convention and electing instead a black Mississippian, John R. Lynch. But the well-oiled Blaine steamroller quickly squashed the upstart opposition. A harbinger came at one point early on when the mere mention of their hero's name sent the "Blainiacs" into a frenzy that ignited a spontaneous outburst on the convention floor that lasted a full twenty minutes. At the moment that Blaine's nomination as the party's candidate was announced, William McKinley rushed to Roosevelt's seat "to urge him to make a unity speech in favor of Blaine." A disappointed Roosevelt flatly refused. In the end, however, unlike a number of other Eastern Republicans, both Roosevelt and Lodge supported the party's nominee and actively campaigned for James G. Blaine. Ambitious, but above all realistic, the two young men chose to become what the party's seasoned standard-bearer already was—professional politicians.[11]

Blaine's nomination came at a cost. Independent Republicans (or "mugwumps" as they were derisively labeled, supposedly because of their indecisiveness—their mugs on one side of the fence and their wumps on the other) bolted and refused to support the party's nominee. The mugwumps, who were concentrated in the Northeast states, especially in New England among the Massachusetts elite and Boston Brahmins, flocked to the banner of the reform-minded Democrat, Grover Cleveland, a candidate believed to be unsullied by political or personal corruption. That New England aristocrats and Harvard intellectuals found him distasteful surely came as no surprise to the sophisticated and experienced politician Blaine. For years he and his family had been snubbed socially and politically by the likes of Henry and Clover Adams, who despised the Plumed Knight and all that he represented. When the anonymously authored novel *Democracy*, which satirized the American democratic process, was published in the United States in March 1880, it was readily apparent that the main villain, the corrupt Senator Silas P. Ratcliffe of Illinois, was a thinly disguised version of James G. Blaine. Most scholars attribute the novel to Henry Adams, but when it first appeared the angry and wounded Senator Blaine identified Clover Adams as the likely author. The Adamses were delighted at Blaine's squirming discomfort. When Henry heard of Blaine's charge that his wife had written the book, he chortled to a friend: "You know how I have always admired Mr. Blaine's powers of invention!"[12]

Initially, Blaine appeared unfazed by the desertion of the mugwumps. The Maine Republican was honored to be his party's standard-bearer in the 1884 presidential campaign and his extended family gloried in the father's nomination. More than a half-century later, his daughter Margaret Blaine Damrosch recalled getting a phone call as a child that still was the "high spot" of her life. Reminiscing about her father's career in 1938 on the occasion when the community leaders of West Brownsville, Pennsylvania were honoring the town's illustrious native son, Mrs. Damrosch wrote: "How I sped from our telephone (the telephone was a new invention then and very recently installed on the second floor of our old Augusta house) to throw myself into his arms, under our old Augusta apple tree, in June 1884, shouting and sobbing 'Father, father you are nominated.'" Mrs. Blaine and the rest of the Augusta household were equally proud and elated, although several months later the family's joy at winning the nomination would turn to the bitter disappointment of defeat in the general election.[13]

In the late nineteenth century, it was customary for a formal party delegation to journey to the candidate's home shortly after the convention to inform him officially of his nomination. Upon receiving word of his nomination from the delegation, James G. Blaine issued an acceptance letter that outlined the main goals of his upcoming campaign. As he earlier had advised his friend James A. Garfield to do in the successful 1880 presidential race, Blaine folded up the "bloody shirt" and laid it away, deciding instead to champion the cause of protectionism. For his own run at the White House, candidate Blaine explicitly coupled the protective tariff with his set of foreign policy blueprints that outlined the advantages of overseas economic expansion, especially in the markets of Latin American neighbors. Blaine called for a revival of the Pan-American project that he had inaugurated as secretary of state and sounded the familiar theme that hemispheric peace would bring extended commerce and common prosperity. The belief that "our foreign relations favor our domestic development" was at the heart of his message to the American electorate.

Blaine sounded one or two other familiar refrains in his acceptance letter. He confidently reiterated his prediction that a glorious national destiny awaited the United States, and to prepare for that era of greatness, "Our foreign policy should be an American policy in its broadest and most comprehensive sense—a policy of peace, of friendship, of commercial enlargement. The name of *American,* which belongs to us in our National capacity, must always exalt the just pride of patriotism." Candidate Blaine also highlighted another feature of his idealized view of national destiny. For more than a decade, he had called for an elevated standard of citizenship for all Americans, based upon dignity, equality, and respect for personal liberty. On two career-defining occasions, at the onset of the Grant administration and again at the time of the nation's centennial celebration in 1876, Blaine had expressed this compelling vision of the American dream. Recognizing that the quest for equality of treatment remained unfulfilled in the mid-1880s, he again demanded that citizenship in "the Republic must be the panoply and safeguard of him who wears it. The American citizen, rich or poor, native or naturalized, white or colored, must everywhere walk secure in his personal and civil rights."[14]

Mindful that charges of political corruption and calls to end the excesses of patronage would loom large in the campaign, Blaine recommended impartial, nonpartisan appointments in the consular service. Evoking imperial imagery designed to capture the attention of the nation's business community, Blaine proclaimed, "Consuls should be commercial sentinels—encircling the globe with watchfulness for their country's interests." Then, in an obvious nod to civil service reformers, the Republican candidate noted that making consular appointments based on "intelligence and competency" was a matter of "great public concern. No man should be appointed to an American consulate who is not well instructed in the history and resources of his own country, and in the requirements and language of commerce in the country to which he is sent." Blaine also urged that the "same rule should be applied even more rigidly to Secretaries of Legation in our Diplomatic service" because the American "people have the right to the most efficient agents in the discharge of public business." These recommendations, the former secretary of state explained, were intended to instill professionalism in the consular and diplomatic service as well as to promote the expansion of American overseas commerce.[15]

Shipbuilder and entrepreneur John Roach was one member of the business and industrial elite who heartily endorsed his old ally's presidential candidacy and program of commercial expansion. Almost immediately after Blaine's nomination, Roach praised his friend for being "the only man" in public office in the early 1880s who saw "we should need a market for our surplus products" and who understood that the nations of South America held out the best prospects for increased trade with the United States. "Yours was not a policy of blood or destruction of life," Roach observed, "but it was one in the interest of the American farmer, manufacturer, and mechanic." Of course, Great Britain understood this and "sees in the Chicago platform and you as its standard-bearer, the handwriting on the wall . . . she sees with your election she is likely to lose her hold on the United States market, and then with your South American policy carried out, the markets of Brazil, Peru, Chili, River Platte and others lost to her. Do you wonder that she is interested? This accounts largely for those attacks on your private character and public policy." Another Blaine supporter and an obvious foreign policy protégé, future Secretary of State John Hay, was equally amused by the nervous British response when he only half-jokingly reported that "England would consider your nomination as a declaration of war."[16]

John Hay obviously exaggerated the nature and extent of the British response. But John Roach was deadly serious. His uncanny assessment of the British reaction to Blaine's candidacy was more accurate than even he knew. At almost the exact moment Roach was writing Blaine in June 1884, Sir Lionel Sackville-West, the British minister to the United States, wrote his chief, Lord Granville, in London that "there is no doubt that if the nomination of Mr. Blaine results in his election to the Presidency in November next, our relations may become uneasy. Blaine is a personal friend of mine, and I know that he might become dangerous." As both the British diplomat and the American businessman understood, James G. Blaine was "dangerous" to Great Britain because his imperial blueprints posed a challenge and threat to British economic supremacy in the world marketplace.[17]

Blaine and his campaign managers assiduously cultivated the perception among the American public that the British establishment wanted the Republican candidate defeated at the polls. The party press as well as GOP campaign literature highlighted numerous articles from British journals that expressed apprehension and misgivings over Blaine's candidacy. Whitelaw Reid, editor of the *New York Tribune* and leading Republican media flack, concluded that British objections to Blaine hinged on their fear and foreboding that his foreign policy threatened England's global commercial supremacy. In that framework, the Republicans cast the protective tariff debate in an aggressively anti-British mold. Grover Cleveland and the Democrats were labeled as free traders who served the interests of Great Britain. The GOP employed slogans such as "British Gold can't shine in this crowd" and the ever reliable "America for Americans" as expressions of economic nationalism that promised to end the United States' subservience to John Bull. One typical campaign pamphlet described Blaine's foreign policy blueprints as the only plan for an aggressive diplomacy that would prevent Great Britain from lording it over the Americas "as she does over Asia and Africa" and would guarantee that Americans remained "masters of our destinies."[18]

Almost immediately after receiving the GOP presidential nomination, James G. Blaine shed his earlier ambivalence about his candidacy and wholeheartedly plunged into the campaign. Accompanied by the pageantry of countless marching companies, many featuring Plumed Knight legions in full regalia, and the dazzling spectacle of torchlight parades and brilliant fireworks displays, Blaine broke precedent in a presidential canvass by staging a six-week campaign tour of the Northeast and Midwest. Boarding a train in Massachusetts in mid-September after speaking at the Worcester Agricultural Fair, he barnstormed through nine states and gave more than four hundred speeches to large, enthusiastic crowds. Keeping his message simple and concise, Blaine repeatedly linked protectionism to continued national prosperity. In his first major address west of the Hudson River, in Hamilton, Ohio, the Republican standard-bearer tied the stupendous economic growth and material progress of the United States in the post–Civil War era directly to the protective tariff. Then in Grafton, West Virginia, Blaine sounded another of his recurrent themes, by "inviting the whole South to join in a great National movement which shall in fact and in feeling, as well as in form, make us a people with one union, one Constitution, one destiny." This frenetic campaign

Campaign Flag. Courtesy of the Maine State Museum.

swing was in sharp contrast to the more traditional and widely accepted strategy of the Democratic contender, Grover Cleveland, who
as governor of New York stayed at home in Albany and presented only
two set speeches.[19]

Blaine also had strong support on the campaign trail from a number of prominent Republicans, including Senator Benjamin Harrison
of Indiana. Harrison gave the keynote address at the party ratification
ceremonies in the nation's capital. The Hoosier senator, anticipating
the opposition's charges of jingoism and foreign policy bungling, unabashedly equated Blaine's statesmanship with that of the preeminent
European leaders of the day, Germany's chancellor, Otto von Bismarck, and Great Britain's prime minister, William E. Gladstone. Later
that summer the Indiana senator also kicked off the Republican national campaign in Indianapolis with another rousing endorsement of
the party's presidential candidate. In late August, before Blaine began
his extensive campaign swing, Harrison embarked by train for Maine
to discuss campaign strategy with the GOP nominee and to stump for
the Republican ticket prior to the mid-September election in that state.
(Maine voted early because there was no nationwide date set aside for
federal elections in the nineteenth century, giving rise to the false ad-
age about American presidential elections, that "as Maine goes, so
goes the nation.")

Among politicians in-the-know at the time, it was generally
assumed that the central goal of Harrison's trek to Maine, where he

spent the weekend with the Blaine family at their Augusta home consulting at length with the candidate, was not to plan grand campaign strategy, but to map out a specific legal and political response to a scurrilous attack by an Indiana newspaper. The Democratic *Sentinel* of Indianapolis charged that the Blaines had been married on March 29, 1851, and that their son had been born on June 18, 1851. It was evident, according to the *Sentinel*, that Mr. Blaine was a scoundrel who betrayed an innocent girl and only "married her at the muzzle of a shotgun." Actually, Harriet Stanwood and James G. Blaine were married in Kentucky on June 30, 1850, but the ceremony was open to legal scrutiny because the groom had neglected to get a proper marriage license. Months later, realizing that their Kentucky marriage might be invalid, the Blaines went through another ceremony in Pittsburgh, Pennsylvania, on March 29, 1851. When the scandalous charges about his marriage date first surfaced, an outraged Blaine hired Benjamin Harrison as his attorney and instructed him to bring criminal charges for libel against the newspaper. Ultimately, however, the Republican candidate, with Harrison's encouragement, dropped the libel suit and went on with the campaign.

The "shot-gun marriage" brouhaha was just one of a number of such sensationalist sideshows in a presidential campaign that many have labeled the dirtiest and vilest waged in the late nineteenth century. For their part, the Democrats saw the attack on Blaine's marital history as an eye-for-an-eye payback for an earlier Republican revelation that as a young man Grover Cleveland had fathered an illegitimate child. Both sets of titillating allegations about the private lives and personal morality of the candidates were ill timed and appeared early enough in the campaign for each man to recover politically. Arguably, had the story of Cleveland's sexual liaison with the widow Maria Halpin, a Buffalo, New York, shop clerk, come out sooner, the New York governor would not have received his party's nomination, and had it come out in late October during the last two weeks of the campaign, Cleveland probably would have lost the election. But in 1884 neither major party had mastered the art of the "October surprise," whereby outrageous charges or new revelations about a candidate are made at the last minute, at a point in the campaign too late to be successfully denied or credibly refuted. In their haste to smear the morally upright Cleveland, Blaine and his advisers missed the opportunity to launch an October surprise, a political ploy that now has become an almost standard feature of American presidential campaigns.

Ironically, the October surprise that did appear in 1884 was completely unplanned and totally unexpected by either party's campaign staff, but it nonetheless proved disastrous to James G. Blaine and his chances of winning the election. After his long and arduous speaking tour of the Midwest, a weary Blaine stopped in the pivotal state of New York on the way back to his home in Augusta, Maine. In New York City, on October 29, at a gathering of Protestant ministers, the Reverend Samuel D. Burchard addressed the candidate and assured him that: "We are Republicans, and don't propose to leave our party and identify ourselves with the party whose antecedents have been rum, Romanism, and rebellion. We are loyal to our flag. We are loyal to you." An exhausted Blaine had lost his sense of judgment and failed to disclaim Burchard's "rum, Romanism, and rebellion" alliteration on the spot. The Democrats immediately pounced on the abusive phrase, realizing it was a political bombshell. The next Sunday morning thousands of flyers quoting the bigoted remark were handed out at Catholic churches across the nation. Blaine unequivocally disowned Burchard's statement on November 1, but it was too late. The damaging fallout from this inadvertent October surprise killed the Republican ticket's chances, especially among Irish Catholics. Blaine lost New York and its thirty-six electoral votes by fewer than 1,200 votes, which in turn cost him the national election.

Blaine initially accepted his heartbreaking loss at the polls with stoic calm, reminding friends he had not wanted the nomination in the first place. Mrs. Harriet Blaine, however, said the narrow defeat was "all a horror to me," and admitted that the agony of the election night "will never go out of my memory." After some reflection on what had gone wrong, her husband observed to a friend that, "I should have carried New York by 10,000 if the weather had been clear on election day and Dr. Burchard had been doing missionary work in Asia Minor or Cochin China" (the southern region of present-day Vietnam). Blaine's appraisal of the Burchard fiasco was shared by his confidant, *New York Tribune* editor Whitelaw Reid, who wrote Republican loyalist John Hay: "Don't deceive yourself about Burchard, however. He did defeat us. He did more than that. He took ten thousand votes away from us in this city and Brooklyn." A few Blaine diehards, notably railroad magnate Chauncey Depew, believed the Democrats had stolen the election by liberally buying votes in key New York precincts. Nearly a half-century later, in 1932, the loss still rankled Edwin Doak Mead, a Massachusetts reformer who had not defected to the mugwumps. Thinking back to that bitter defeat, an aged Mead confessed:

"My blood boils to this day at remembrance of the groundless and malignant charges which were hurled against Mr. Blaine by the mugwump crowd during that summer and autumn."[20]

A few weeks after the election, James G. Blaine publicly offered an extensive explanation for the GOP's first loss of the White House since Lincoln's victory in 1860. The "bloody shirt" may have been folded away during the campaign, but it reappeared in the defeated candidate's speech to a large number of Republican friends outside his Augusta home. Speaking as "a loyal and devoted American," Blaine thought the transfer of political power to the South was a "Great National misfortune." He believed that in the Southern states the "colored population almost to a man desire to support the Republican party, but by a system of reckless intimidation, and by violence and murder whenever violence and murder are required, they are absolutely deprived of political power." Not only was the colored population disenfranchised through violence and intimidation, but the political power of six million blacks was transferred to the white population of the South, which meant that Southern white men were "exerting just double the political power of the white men in the Northern States." Blaine's argument revealed the Republican party's dilemma concerning suffrage for the black population in the South— justice demanded that former slaves be enfranchised, but that entailed the risk that black political power would be controlled by former slave owners and Southern white men.[21]

Blaine's election postmortem may easily be dismissed as yet another of his predictable "bloody shirt" tactics, but in this case such a dismissal both ignores the validity of Blaine's analysis and overlooks the commitment to racial justice he and many other Republicans shared in the post–Civil War era. They confronted a serious political challenge: how to guarantee freed blacks the rights of citizenship and prevent them from being disenfranchised by racist Southern whites? In the late 1860s, at the time the Fourteenth Amendment was being crafted, Blaine recognized this problem and hoped that his modification of the amendment contained in Section 2, which would reduce a state's representation in proportion to the number of citizens whose rights were denied or abridged on the basis of race or color, would prevent the disenfranchisement of blacks in the South and, not incidentally, produce a bloc of black voters loyal to the Republican party. However, to preserve sectional unity after Reconstruction, Republicans shied away from seeking federal enforcement of this provision of the Fourteenth Amendment, although many, including Theodore Roosevelt and Frederick Douglass, believed that had Southern blacks been allowed to vote in 1884, Blaine would have been elected.

But Blaine did not wallow in self-pity after his narrow defeat. Nor was he politically immobilized by a "we wuz robbed" syndrome. He retained his standing as Mr. Republican and remained the intellectual leader of the party on foreign policy and the tariff. As he had done after the shock of Garfield's murder, Blaine went on the offensive to preserve the essence of his imperial blueprints. Again he targeted the diplomacy of the outgoing Arthur administration, which, during its frenetic last months in office, outdid even Blaine in the audacity of its expansionist foreign policy. Undoubtedly disappointed at failing to receive renomination, and probably still smarting from Blaine's earlier harsh criticism of the administration's policies, neither President Chester A. Arthur nor Secretary of State Frederick Frelinghuysen supported the presidential campaign of their despised intraparty rival. Instead, they launched a series of imperial initiatives designed to establish U.S. hegemony in Central America and the Caribbean and to extend American influence to a new frontier in the heart of the African continent.

Only a few months before the Democrat Grover Cleveland was to enter the White House, the Arthur administration submitted for Senate approval an economic expansionist package of reciprocity agreements signed with the Dominican Republic and with Spain for Cuba and Puerto Rico. In addition, Arthur and Freylinghuysen sought ratification of a Nicaraguan canal treaty, which would establish Nicaragua as a U.S. protectorate in return for an American-controlled isthmian waterway. Earlier in the election year, Secretary Frelinghuysen had sent an American delegate, John Kasson, to a Berlin conference called by German Chancellor Otto von Bismarck to negotiate a peaceful solution to European competition for control of the Congo. In the treaty drawn up at the conference, Kasson achieved the Arthur administration's goal of preserving an open door for American commercial interests in the Congo. Although these initiatives by the outgoing Arthur administration appeared to be consistent with Blaine's imperial agenda, he opposed most of these measures, especially the Congo treaty. Blaine criticized his fellow Republicans for signing the treaty because such a course in Africa invited British and general European involvement in the Western Hemisphere, which, in turn, threatened the Monroe Doctrine. In December 1884, Blaine expressed his concerns to the British minister to the United States, Sir Lionel Sackville-West: "How can we maintain the Monroe Doctrine when we take part in conferences on the internal affairs of other continents?" For Blaine, United States meddling in Africa only invited European meddling in the Americas.[22]

The defeated Republican candidate's reservations about the wisdom of the Congo treaty were shared by the incoming Cleveland administration. Cleveland withdrew the treaty from the Senate and quickly scotched both the Nicaragua canal treaty and the Arthur-Frelinghuysen package of reciprocity treaties as well. On purely partisan grounds, Democratic opposition to such an activist Republican diplomacy was to be expected. But why did Mr. Republican oppose the foreign policy actions of fellow Republicans, all of which, with the exception of the plunge into Africa, were pages right out of his blueprint portfolio? An obvious answer was Blaine's bitterness at the utter failure of President Arthur and Secretary Frelinghuysen to support him during the election campaign. Another explanation for his pique was that a proud and temperamental Blaine did not wish to be upstaged, either politically or diplomatically. Perhaps, though, the most important factor in his opposition to the Arthur program was that Blaine's imperial designs had limits. He objected to any diplomatic overtures, whether from within his own party or emanating from the opposition, that recklessly jeopardized future American hegemony in the Western Hemisphere. The man who had been ridiculed in the press as "Jingo Jim" was in reality a restrained, cautious, and responsible spokesman for the nation's imperial destiny.

However, Blaine's criticism aside, there was little doubt that the Arthur administration had helped keep Pan-Americanism alive and that, overall, its agenda was beneficial in the long term to the promotion of Blaine's Latin American project. Clearly, President Arthur and Secretary of State Frelinghuysen sustained the policy of previous Republican administrations by attempting to establish the United States' commercial hegemony in the Western Hemisphere. Despite the intense intraparty bickering, a large measure of consensus existed within the GOP ranks on the issues of economic expansion and the need for foreign markets to alleviate economic depression. By attempting to establish commercial hegemony in the Western Hemisphere, Republicans of all stripes and factions were active economic nationalists who honored the Monroe Doctrine and acted on the options for American empire implicit in that policy. Key European rivals well understood that the Monroe Doctrine and the slogan "America for Americans" meant in truth nothing less than "the Americas for the United States."

An obvious example of this GOP foreign policy consensus on overseas economic expansion and of the influence of Blaine's ideas on

Pan-Americanism came in the summer of 1884 when Secretary Freling-huysen appointed, with congressional approval and funding, a Central and South American Commission. The commission—George H. Sharpe; Solon O. Thatcher; Thomas C. Reynolds, who spoke Spanish; and William E. Curtis, as secretary—visited several Latin American countries and solicited views from businessmen and merchants on how to improve hemispheric trade. In addition to traveling to countries such as Venezuela, where the citizens warmly greeted them, the commissioners also took the pulse of the U.S. business community by hosting receptions in a number of cities, including New York, Philadelphia, New Orleans, and San Francisco. From the testimonies of countless political, business, industrial, and agricultural spokesmen, it became clear to the commissioners that these leaders accepted as a basic premise the proposition that the United States needed overseas markets to prevent economic and social disaster. The commission filed an extensive report that included numerous suggestions and recommendations for American producers and exporters on how to capture Latin American markets. Although the Cleveland administration failed to act on these recommendations, the commission's report was a valuable reference for future use by economic expansionists, including James G. Blaine and his faithful cadre of supporters in Congress.

Among his strongest congressional loyalists were the two Republican senators from his home state of Maine, William P. Frye and Eugene Hale, both of whom served in the Senate for thirty years (1881–1911) and projected Blaine's imperial agenda into the twentieth century. Until Blaine's death in 1893, the three men were in close contact through frequent correspondence and intermittent personal meetings. On occasion, Blaine even drafted speeches for his two protégés on the virtues of Pan-Americanism and the necessity of expanded trade with Latin America. As a member of the Foreign Relations Committee, Senator Frye was the more active of the pair, a regular wheelhorse in harness to overseas economic expansion and the Pan-American ideal of peaceful relations among the nations of the hemisphere. Frye fought for the renewal of the Hawaiian reciprocity treaty and, with the backing of other Blaine allies on the Foreign Relations Committee, kept alive proposals for a Pan-American conference. His efforts paid off in 1888, when the House and Senate passed resolutions authorizing the president to arrange a Pan-American conference to promote hemispheric peace and reciprocal commercial relations. The Pan-American Congress did not meet until 1889, after Benjamin Harrison was in office, and, fittingly, was presided over by the new secretary of state, James G. Blaine.

Prior to both the meeting of the Pan-American conference and the creation of the Pan-American Union, many Latin Americans endorsed the general principles embodied in Blaine's hemispheric project. Some South American leaders may have been suspicious of the project's paternalistic and hegemonic implications, but a number of others initially endorsed the call for peaceful arbitration of disputes, the proposals for economic development, and the plans for the creation of a transportation infrastructure within the hemisphere. In fact, one Central American leader, Justo Rufino Barrios of Guatemala, looked upon Blaine as his country's savior in its border dispute with its larger neighbor, Mexico. During a visit to Washington in July 1882, the Guatemalan president met with Walker Blaine, offering high praise for the elder Blaine's Latin American diplomacy. As Walker later reported to his father, President Barrios said "many most flattering things, among others that he had your picture in his house in Guatemala." Undoubtedly, not all Latin Americans were as effusive in their appraisals of Blaine, but many were willing to give him and his Pan-Americanism the benefit of the doubt until convinced otherwise.[23]

Although Mr. Republican retained a high public profile in the years immediately following his wrenching defeat in the 1884 election, Blaine apparently had decided never again to make a run for the White House. Instead, his imperial blueprints took precedence, and, as the acknowledged architect of empire, Blaine seemed intent on having another chance to implement his plans. In addition to the coordinated lobbying efforts in Congress on behalf of his foreign policy agenda, private citizen Blaine continued to supply articles on topics of the day to Whitelaw Reid's *New York Tribune* and remained in demand as a public speaker. There was a distinct pattern to the line of argument in his public presentations on the podium and in the press as he aggressively sought to make the protective tariff the ground upon which the next presidential canvass would be fought. Perhaps his most comprehensive statement on the connection between protectionism and his imperial blueprints came in late October 1886, when he was campaigning in Pennsylvania for the Republican candidate for governor. In a speech replete with overtones of national power and national destiny, Blaine proudly told his audience of ten thousand people, mostly workingmen, that the protective tariff was the key to victory in the contest for global empire: "We have now run the race with free trade Great Britain for a quarter of a century and the wealth of that nation is not now estimated as double that of this country. It is not even equal to ours. The wealth of the United States today exceeds that of Great

Britain by $10,000,000,000. (Cheers.) If the free trade policy which the Democratic Party under Southern lead imposed upon the United States and which was changed by the election of Abraham Lincoln had continued, does any man suppose we should have overtaken Great Britain in the race for development and empire?"[24]

Blaine's continued presence on the national scene as the major spokesman for the GOP, along with his persistent emphasis on a protectionist policy being crucial to the nation's future economic prosperity and growth, encouraged his most ardent supporters to hope he was preparing to seek the Republican nomination in 1888. Early on, two of his most faithful lieutenants, John Hay and Whitelaw Reid, privately discussed the viability of a Blaine candidacy, and both came to believe he would be nominated and would be able to defeat Cleveland in a rematch. As the public and private pressure to make another run for the presidency began to build, the enigmatic Blaine preempted these machinations by embarking on an extended holiday in Europe. Apparently determined to resist appeals that he seek the nomination, Blaine, with his wife and two of his daughters, sailed from New York for England on June 7, 1887, aboard a North German Lloyd liner. At the pier to see them off were the Blaine sons, Walker, Emmons, and young James. Several weeks later, on August 15, a relaxed Blaine happily reported from London, "I have lost sight of politics."[25]

American politics, however, had not lost sight of James G. Blaine. Speculation about his presidential prospects continued unabated. The *North American Review* ran a series on "Possible Presidents," in which Blaine was prominently featured as the leading candidate because he "is a man of genius in the sphere of state-craft." Neither this speculation nor the fawning adulation fazed Blaine. He was thoroughly enjoying himself, attending gala dinners and elegant receptions, highlighted by Queen Victoria's garden party at Buckingham Palace, which was attended by "all England of royalty, nobility, and fashion." At times, even amidst all the glitter and charm of English high society, his intense American nationalism surfaced. After several splendid outings at which he met "all the leading men of both sides," Blaine sensed that the English nobility "fear, hate, dread the influence of the Republic on their own position and privileges." He also turned down an invitation to the Foreign Office, doubting the propriety of being Lord Salisbury's guest after having written disparagingly of the British leader's anti-Union, pro-Confederacy stance during the Civil War. Blaine's antipathy for some of Great Britain's elite was reciprocated by at least two members of the aristocracy, Joseph Chamberlain and Randolph Churchill, both of whom immediately disliked the American visitor after meeting him.[26]

After almost six months of carefree socializing in the British Isles and extended touring on the Continent, Blaine was again drawn into the vortex of American presidential politics. Back in the United States, President Cleveland's annual December message to Congress had ignited a political firestorm by calling for a broad reduction of the existing tariff rates. Blaine was in Paris when he learned of Cleveland's full-scale assault on protectionism. With superb timing, he immediately entered the fray by arranging to be interviewed on the message by the *New York Tribune*'s foreign reporter. The interview, or "Paris Letter," as it became known, was published by the New York newspaper on December 8, 1887, and widely reprinted by the Republican press throughout the country. By noting that London newspapers welcomed the president's message as a free trade manifesto that would open the American market to an onslaught of British goods, Blaine played upon the anti-British nationalism of his countrymen. Whitelaw Reid instinctively sensed that Cleveland's blunder and Blaine's quick response were a godsend for Republicans. In a *Tribune* editorial of December 9, 1887, entitled "The Absent Leader," Reid proclaimed that, "Mr. Blaine in Europe speaks as an American. Mr. Cleveland in America speaks as a British manufacturer, anxious to be admitted without any charge to a share of the best and largest market in the world." From afar, a contented Blaine must have smiled at the realization that he had framed the debate for the upcoming presidential election.[27]

Whether or not it was so intended, Blaine's Paris Letter thrust Maine's favorite son back into the limelight as the leading candidate for the Republican nomination. A barrage of letters from friends implored him to return home and seek the nomination. Editor Reid informed his friend, with a measure of satisfaction, that Henry Cabot Lodge and Theodore Roosevelt, reluctant Blaine supporters in 1884, now favored his nomination "because they are particularly eager to beat the Mugwumps with you." Blaine was unmoved. He and his family remained in Europe and he declined to be a candidate. At the time of the Republican convention in June 1888, the Blaine entourage, accompanied by Andrew Carnegie and his wife, were on a four-week coach trip in Scotland. Four American reporters were tailing the party to see if Blaine might change his mind and become a candidate for the GOP nomination. (This nineteenth-century practice of newspapermen hounding a politician was a forerunner of the late twentieth-century ritual of celebrity stalking by packs of international media photographers known as "paparazzi.") After several days of tailing Blaine, the reporters broke the news of Benjamin Harrison's nomination to him while he was tramping the ruins of Linlithgow castle, birthplace of Mary, Queen of Scots. Meanwhile, the Democrats, as expected, renominated Grover Cleveland.[28]

Upon his triumphal return to the United States in August, Mr. Republican was warmly greeted in New York City by a large crowd. Benjamin Harrison was not among those welcoming him at the pier, but the GOP nominee lost no time in contacting his esteemed friend to court his support on the stump in the fall campaign. Blaine readily complied, both out of party loyalty and the conviction that Harrison shared his imperial vision and a belief in national destiny. Four years earlier, when their roles were reversed and Blaine was the presidential aspirant and Harrison was among the leading speakers on the campaign circuit, the two veteran protectionists had bonded intellectually. Although Blaine was essentially the mentor and Harrison the student in this relationship, the Indianapolis lawyer already had accepted, as a basic premise, the need for overseas commercial expansion and expanded foreign markets for the nation's surplus products. At their meeting in Augusta during Blaine's unsuccessful bid for the White House, ostensibly to discuss the marriage date controversy, the two men shared thoughts on the nation's foreign policy agenda. After the Republican loss in 1884, Harrison did what all savvy politicians do: he prepared for the next election. Inspired by Blaine's imperial blueprints, the Indiana senator spent the Christmas holiday in Washington studying the history of the Monroe Doctrine, reviewing proposals for an American-constructed isthmian canal, and preparing his case for legislation that allocated large expenditures for an expanded, modern navy.

For the remainder of his term in the Senate, Harrison pursued expansionist measures and backed the effort to call a Pan-American conference. During his brief service on the Foreign Relations Committee, he had voted to extend the Hawaiian reciprocity treaty. It was little wonder then that Blaine enthusiastically agreed to campaign for Harrison. At the start of the 1888 presidential campaign, the two expansionists clearly agreed on the future course of American foreign relations. However, they were not, and never would be, soul mates in the way Blaine and Garfield had been. Although he obviously needed Blaine's support to win in the campaign against Cleveland, the high-voiced, diminutive Harrison, known as "Little Ben" and reputed to be a cold fish, was jealous and wary of the more charming and magnetic

Plumed Knight. But Blaine did what was expected and worked tirelessly for the Republican ticket. Once again, he added excitement to the campaign, inspiring parades and fireworks and mesmerizing audiences at mass public meetings with his magnificent oratory. The Republicans effectively used the tariff issue and the ever-popular slogan "America for Americans—No Free Trade" to nail down the image of the Democrats as the pro-British party. Even with Blaine's help and the blatant pandering to anti-British nationalism, Harrison barely squeaked past Grover Cleveland in November. He won the electoral vote by a count of 233 to 168, but Cleveland had a one hundred thousand plurality in the popular vote.

Once victory was secured, Blaine made little secret of the fact that he wished to head the State Department in the new administration. Shortly after the election, he wrote Whitelaw Reid: "I see no objection to you saying to any one that I will take the Secy State-ship if offered to me." Several of his friends pressed the matter, urging the new president to appoint Blaine to his cabinet as secretary of state. Harrison would not be crowded and moved cautiously because he wished to preclude being overshadowed by his more illustrious Republican ally. Little Ben adroitly took every precaution to assert that he was in control and that if Blaine were in the cabinet, he would be kept on a short leash. On January 17, 1889, President Harrison ended the suspense and formally offered James G. Blaine the position of secretary of state. Blaine gladly accepted what he so ardently desired.[29]

The arrival of President Harrison's official invitation to join his cabinet caused unbridled joy and excitement in the Blaine family household. Harriet Blaine exclaimed to her youngest son, Jamie, "I thrill when I think of the part your Father may play in the Future of this country." After more than seven years as a private citizen, James G. Blaine happily looked forward to reentering public life and government service. He immediately prepared to resume his old duties at State by studying maps and reviewing background information about the crisis with Germany and Great Britain over Samoa, at one point even reading aloud to one of his sons about the strategic and commercial importance of those remote Pacific islands more than half a globe away. A proven political survivor who overcame the ignominy of forced resignation from the State Department and the agony of defeat in 1884, a satisfied Blaine no longer dreamed of becoming president of the United States. His ambition now was limited to returning to Washington as secretary of state, with the opportunity to implement his imperial blueprints and fulfill the nation's destiny.[30]

Notes

1. Mrs. James G. Blaine to M., February 2, 1882, in *Letters of Mrs. James G. Blaine,* ed. Harriet S. Blaine Beale, 2 vols. (New York: Duffield and Company, 1908), 1:296–97.

2. *New York Tribune,* February 4, 1882.

3. James G. Blaine, "The South American Policy of the Garfield Administration," *Chicago Weekly Magazine,* September 16, 1882, 1–3. Kipling published his poem, "The White Man's Burden," in 1899.

4. Mrs. James G. Blaine to Margaret Blaine, December 25, 1881, in *Letters,* 276.

5. Julia B. Foraker, *I Would Live It Again, Memories of a Vivid Life* (New York: Harper and Brothers Publishers, 1932), 80–1.

6. Mrs. James G. Blaine to Margaret Blaine, March 1, 1882, in *Letters,* 317.

7. Alfred E. Eckes, Jr., *Opening America's Market: U.S. Foreign Trade Policy Since 1776* (Chapel Hill: University of North Carolina Press, 1995), 69.

8. James G. Blaine to Allison, February 10, 1883, William B. Allison Papers, State Historical Society of Iowa; Blaine to Morrill, July 10, 1883, Justin Morrill Papers, Library of Congress; Joseph A. Fry, *John Tyler Morgan and the Search for Southern Autonomy* (Knoxville: University of Tennessee Press, 1992), 82.

9. Charles W. Calhoun, *Gilded Age Cato: The Life of Walter Q. Gresham* (Lexington: University Press of Kentucky, 1988), 75.

10. Murat Halstead, "The Defeat of Blaine for the Presidency," *McClure's Magazine,* January 1896, 159–172.

11. Nathan Miller, *Theodore Roosevelt, A Life* (New York: William Morrow and Company, 1992), 158–61.

12. Otto Friedrich, *Clover* (New York: Simon and Schuster, 1979), 240.

13. Margaret Blaine Damrosch to H.H. Hain, October 4, 1938, Blaine Papers, Library of Congress.

14. "Mr. Blaine's Letter Accepting the Republican Nomination for the Presidency in 1884," in James G. Blaine, *Political Discussions: Legislative, Diplomatic and Popular* (Norwich, CT: Henry Bill Publishing Company, 1887), 420–34.

15. Ibid., 432.

16. John Roach to Blaine, June 12, 1884, in Gail Hamilton, *Biography of James G. Blaine* (Norwich, CT: Henry Bill Publishing Company, 1895), 627–28; John Hay to Blaine, June 7, 1884, Blaine Papers, Library of Congress.

17. Sir Lionel Sackville-West to Granville, June 10, 1884, in Paul Knaplund and Carolyn M. Clewes, *Private Letters from the British Embassy in Washington to the Foreign Secretary Lord Granville, 1880–1885,* Annual Report of the American Historical Association, 3 vols. 1941 (Washington, DC: Government Printing Office, 1942), 1:178.

18. Edward P. Crapol, *America for Americans: Economic Nationalism and Anglophobia in the Late Nineteenth Century* (Westport, CT: Greenwood Press, 1973), 86; James Morris Morgan, *America's Egypt, Mr. Blaine's Foreign Policy* (New York: Herman Bartsch, Printer, 1884), 5.

19. Blaine, *Political Discussions,* 435–65.

20. Mrs. James G. Blaine to Alice Blaine Coppinger, November 30, 1884, in *Letters,* 2:120–21; Blaine quoted in Mark D. Hirsch, "Election of 1884," in *History of American Presidential Elections, 1789–1968,* ed. Arthur M. Schlesinger, Jr.,

and Fred L. Israel 4 vols. (New York: Chelsea House Publishers, 1971), 2:1581; Reid to John Hay, December 1, 1884, in Royal Cortissoz, *The Life of Whitelaw Reid*, 2 vols. (New York: Charles Scribner's Sons, 1921), 2:98; Edwin Doak Mead to Thomas H. Sherman, August 12, 1932, James G. Blaine Papers, Library of Congress.

21. Blaine speech after election, November 18, 1884, in Blaine, *Political Discussions*, 466–71.

22. Blaine quoted in David S. Muzzey, *James G. Blaine: A Political Idol of Other Days* (New York: Dodd, Mead and Company, 1934), 425.

23. Walker Blaine to James G. Blaine, July 25, 1882, in Hamilton, *Biography of Blaine*, 568.

24. *New York Times*, October 20, 1886.

25. Blaine quoted in Hamilton, *Biography of Blaine*, 644.

26. Ibid., 642.

27. *New York Tribune*, December 9, 1887.

28. Muzzey, *Blaine*, 373.

29. Blaine to Reid, November 28, 1888, Whitelaw Reid Papers, Library of Congress.

30. Mrs. James G. Blaine to Jamie Blaine, February 11, 1889, in *Letters*, 2:245.

6

Imperial Statesmanship, 1889–1892

I think there are only three places that are value enough to be taken, that are not continental. One is Hawaii and the others are Cuba and Porto Rico. Cuba and Porto Rico are not now imminent and will not be for a generation. Hawaii may come up for decision at any unexpected hour and I hope we shall be prepared to decide it in the affirmative.
— James G. Blaine, 1891

As the leading architect of late nineteenth-century American empire, James G. Blaine was eager in March, 1889, to return to the secretary of state's office in the recently completed State, War, and Navy Building. After seventeen years of construction, this magnificent imperial structure, which was the largest office building in Washington and among the largest in the world at the time, had been officially dedicated the year before. As a member of the short-lived Garfield administration, Blaine had occupied an office in the unfinished building, and he looked forward to once again having the pleasure of directing the nation's foreign relations from within its splendid walls. During the course of Blaine's second stint as head of the State Department, this Victorian masterpiece was opened to the public and in the early 1890s became a popular stop for tourists, especially during the celebration of national holidays such as the Fourth of July, when the building was festively decorated with flags and red, white, and blue bunting. For millions of Americans, the State, War, and Navy Building became a proud showcase and symbol of American power and glory. For Secretary Blaine, the grand scale of the edifice also boldly proclaimed that an imperial republic had come of age, ready and willing to assume its rightful place in the international arena as one of the world's leading nations.

President-elect Benjamin Harrison shared Blaine's vision of American destiny and greatness and was equally eager and determined to implement an expansionist agenda. There was little mystery as to how Ben Harrison, the "shrewd and unfriendly little lawyer from Indiana," came to command a knowledge of empire: he had been Blaine's pupil for almost a decade, keenly working to master the mentor's imperial blueprints. In the 1884 campaign, Harrison's admiration for Blaine was apparent when he ranked his mentor as a statesman comparable in ability to Europe's finest diplomats. In his letter offering his teacher the position of secretary of state, Harrison forthrightly stated that, "We have already a pretty full understanding of each other's views as to the general policy which should characterize our foreign relations. I am especially interested in the improvement of our relations with the Central and South American states." In happily accepting the offer with its explicit reference to his Pan-American project, Blaine wrote back: "I am glad to find myself in heartiest accord with the principles and policies which you briefly outline for your administration, and I am especially pleased with what you say in regard to Foreign Affairs."[1]

Everything may have appeared rosy at the outset of their heady and exhilarating quest for empire, but Harrison quickly made it clear that his student days were over. As the new president of the United States, Little Ben was to be the boss. He deliberately took his time in making selections for his cabinet and held a tight rein on other executive appointments and patronage in general. Harrison carefully limited the number of Blaine men in his administration and rejected Blaine's request that his son be named first assistant secretary of state. Walker Blaine instead had to settle for a position as the State Department's examiner of claims. Initially, Blaine was not troubled by the changed power relationship with his former pupil. He was a political realist who knew his place, and, over the course of the next three years, he only occasionally overstepped his bounds with the president. In 1889 Blaine was suffering from kidney disease and physically past his prime. No longer as impulsive as he once was, the Plumed Knight had mellowed since 1881 and, to the surprise of many, had become a restrained and responsible imperial statesman.

One incident in particular during the appointments process at the State Department illustrated Secretary Blaine's stature as a seasoned leader who understood the nuances of diplomacy. Among the deluge of patronage requests that flooded into the new secretary of state's office was one from Henry Cabot Lodge on behalf of his friend, Theodore Roosevelt. Because both he and Roosevelt had campaigned hard for Harrison and the GOP in the just-concluded election, the Massachusetts congressman believed Roosevelt deserved to be appointed assistant secretary of state. James G. Blaine's response to Lodge was a classic description of young, ambitious Teddy Roosevelt: "My real trouble in regard to Mr. Roosevelt is that I fear he lacks the repose and patient endurance required in an Assistant Secretary. Mr. Roosevelt is amazingly quick in apprehension. Is there not danger that he might be too quick in execution? I do somehow fear that my sleep at Augusta or Bar Harbor would not be quite as easy and refreshing if so brilliant and aggressive a man had hold of the helm. Matters are constantly occurring which require the most thoughtful concentration and most stubborn inaction. Do *you* think that Mr. T.R.'s temperament would give guaranty of that course?" Lodge had no rebuttal to this devastatingly accurate appraisal of his friend. Understandably, Theodore Roosevelt was disappointed that he had missed the chance to shape the nation's foreign policy under Blaine's tutelage. Years later, however, as assistant secretary of the Navy in the McKinley administration, Roosevelt's aggressive take-charge actions, often without the approval of his superiors, confirmed that Blaine had known his man.[2]

When Secretary Blaine took up his duties at the State Department for a second time, he must have been pleased, even pleasantly surprised, by the underlying continuity and consensus that prevailed in American foreign relations. After three years of diplomatic activity by the Republican administration that had unceremoniously dumped him and scuttled his Pan-American project and after four years of a Democratic administration that had labeled him a reckless jingo and defeated him at the polls, Blaine might have expected that his imperial blueprints would have been discarded or, at the very least, ruthlessly scaled back. Not so. If anything, the Arthur and Cleveland administrations, with the prodding assistance of tenacious expansionists in Congress, bequeathed James G. Blaine the basic outlines of a new paradigm in American diplomacy that closely followed the key features of his imperial blueprints. Or, to use a different, but equally useful metaphor, it was as if Blaine the weaver, after a long absence, had replaced a fellow artisan at the loom and simply picked up the familiar strands in the design and continued weaving in a nearly identical imperial pattern. It may not have been a one-size-fits-all grand imperial design, but the pattern that emerged did display a remarkable continuity and consistency.

Whether the imagery was that of an architect or a weaver, the point to be understood was that Secretary of State Blaine readily picked up

James G. Blaine. Courtesy of the Department of State.

where he left off more than seven years earlier. This was true for American policy in the Caribbean, in Central America and the broader Western Hemisphere, as well as in Hawaii, Samoa, Korea, and throughout the Pacific Rim. Equally important to this basic level of continuity in the pursuit of the nation's destiny in the last decades of the nineteenth century was the fact that Blaine and his star pupil and current boss, President Harrison, shared an imperial vision and were intent on fulfilling their expansionist agenda. Both men were now ready to pursue President Grant's earlier goal of a naval base in the Caribbean, and eager to ensure that the United States would control two of the potentially finest naval stations in the Pacific—Pearl Harbor in Hawaii and Pago Pago in Samoa. But Blaine and Harrison also recognized limitations on their imperial vision, and exclusively focused on the Western Hemisphere and the Pacific. The self-imposed restraints on their imperial agenda became clear when the Harrison administration rejected Portugal's offer of coaling stations in Africa. This decision was consistent with Blaine's earlier objections to American participation in the Berlin conference on the Congo. As President Harrison explained his administration's priorities, it was not "very important for us to secure coaling stations for our men of war in either the European or African possessions of Portugal, but have regarded it as very important that, in the West Indies, in the Pacific islands, South America etc., we should have such stations."[3]

Korea provided one of the first opportunities the new secretary of state had to implement his blueprints and sustain the continuity of his earlier goals for the Pacific Rim. As head of the State Department in the Garfield administration, Blaine had been responsible for sending Admiral Robert W. Shufeldt to negotiate the United States' first commercial treaty with the Hermit Kingdom, which the naval officer accomplished in 1882. In addition to opening Korea to the West, Blaine hoped to undermine Chinese dominance over the Korean kingdom. Attaining some autonomy for Korea and an open door for American interests remained priorities for Blaine, and with those objectives in mind, he offered Shufeldt the post of minister to China in June 1889. Unwilling to give up his retired admiral's pension, Shufeldt declined. Undaunted, Secretary Blaine turned elsewhere for help in implementing a policy that sought Korea's independence from China.

American missionaries, merchants, and entrepreneurs had benefited from Shufeldt's opening of the Hermit Kingdom. Perhaps no one gained more than Dr. Horace Allen, the first Protestant missionary to serve in Korea and a prototype of the nineteenth-century American advance man for empire. Allen, claiming to be Blaine's friend and an acquaintance of President Harrison's family, relentlessly combined soul-saving with moneymaking. Intent on raising capital from American investors to exploit Korea's vast mineral resources, Allen approached Secretary Blaine for help. After considering the Allen proposal, Blaine promised his friend that, if American businessmen obtained mining concessions from Korean authorities, the U.S. government would "guarantee the parties—if of good standing—to take measures looking to the success of their work." In pursuit of his, and the president's, strategic objectives in the Pacific Rim, the secretary of state also informed Allen that the Harrison administration would ask Korea for a coaling station for the U.S. Navy, which might, in turn, ward off the Russians and reduce Chinese influence on the Korean peninsula. Finally, Blaine selected Horace Allen as the man to guide his Korean policy and appointed him secretary of the American legation in Seoul. Blaine's ambitious moves in Korea came to very little. The United States did not get a coaling facility, and it took almost five years for Allen and his business partners to profit from Korea's northern gold mines, which were among the richest in Asia.[4]

Blaine had better luck in Samoa. His predecessor, Secretary of State Thomas Bayard, had bequeathed the Republicans an unresolved dispute over Samoan autonomy among the United States, Great Britain, and Germany. Secretary-designate Blaine had prepared himself for this contingency by poring over maps of the distant Pacific islands and reviewing the relevant diplomatic correspondence. Just before Benjamin Harrison was sworn in, Germany's chancellor, Otto von Bismarck, suggested the three powers, in a resumption of an earlier unsuccessful conference in Washington, meet in Berlin to resolve the issue. The lame duck Cleveland-Bayard team accepted the invitation, but left the appointment of delegates and the details of participation in the conference to the incoming Harrison administration. In formulating their strategy for the upcoming meeting, Harrison and Blaine accepted Bayard's basic argument favoring equal three-power control to guarantee Samoan autonomy, but the two men took an even stronger stance than the Democrats had previously outlined. Blaine's instructions to the newly selected delegates to the Berlin Samoan conference confirmed the need for a naval station at Pago Pago and forcefully asserted that the United States' interest in the Pacific was "steadily increasing" and that American trade with Asia was growing "largely and rapidly." These new developments, coupled with the certainty of an early opening of an isthmian canal under American auspices, dictated that "this Government cannot accept even temporary subordination" of its expanding role in the Pacific.[5]

At first glance, it appeared that the new secretary of state was being transparently inconsistent in agreeing to participate in an international conference in the heart of Europe. Had not Blaine from 1884 to 1885 publicly opposed American involvement in just such a conference on the Congo, in the same European city? True enough, but in Blaine's mind the Congo conference had represented a threat to the Monroe Doctrine and American hegemony in the Western Hemisphere, whereas Samoa was a projected outpost of American power in the Pacific Rim and within the legitimate boundaries of his imperial blueprints. He and a host of nineteenth-century Americans, including the poet Walt Whitman, believed the popular expansionist dictum, coined a century earlier by an English clergyman, that "westward the course of empire takes its way." In addition, the United States possessed the right to construct a naval station in the islands and had existing obligations to guarantee native sovereignty on the basis of a treaty of friendship and commerce with Samoa, unanimously ratified by the Senate in 1878 when James G. Blaine was Maine's junior senator.

As a result of the hard-line stance he framed for the American delegation to the conference, Secretary Blaine, with unflagging support from President Harrison, satisfactorily resolved the crisis by accepting a tripartite power-sharing arrangement that guaranteed Samoan autonomy. He also solidified America's claim to and control of the splendid harbor of Pago Pago. The agreement proved only a temporary solution, however: ten years later, in 1899, the islands were partitioned between the United States and Germany. Arguably, James G. Blaine valiantly had crossed diplomatic swords with the mighty Bismarck. Among Americans and Europeans, the perception was that the United States had triumphed and that the American secretary of state had faced down the "Iron Chancellor." However, the public's assessment was not entirely accurate. As one American delegate to the conference admitted, the German leader voluntarily and magnanimously decided to undo "a great wrong." Nonetheless, Blaine basked in the momentary glow of victory. In the eyes of the world, the famed Plumed Knight had tested and verified Benjamin Harrison's belief that the American statesman was the equal of the great Bismarck. When Kaiser Wilhelm II abruptly dismissed Bismarck the following year, Blaine, who knew he was not in the same league as the legendary Iron Chancellor, incredulously wrote a friend: "The most remarkable man that has appeared on the continent of Europe since the first Napoleon—what an insufferable fool that young Emperor must be."[6]

The Samoa agreement may have demonstrated anew that the United States was a major player on the international scene, but some observers believed the treaty was a dangerous departure from the nation's traditional policy of nonentanglement. Apparently, Blaine had similar reservations. He initially informed the conference delegates that binding the United States to such an agreement with Britain and Germany was not "in harmony with the established policy of this Government." In the end, however, the American secretary accepted the entangling arrangement of three-power control as the only way to end the impasse and reach accord with Germany and Great Britain. Actually, the precedent for accepting responsibility for securing and protecting another people's autonomy had been set in 1882 with Shufeldt's treaty with Korea, which Blaine originally had instigated. Article 1 of that treaty pledged the United States to exert its "good offices" to protect Korean sovereignty. Moreover, the 1889 tripartite agreement was virtually identical to what Secretary Bayard had proposed two years earlier. Despite Blaine's hand-wringing over entangling alliances, from a European perspective there was little difference between the Democrats and Republicans when it came to pursuing American expansionist goals in the Pacific Rim. Once again, a vision of national destiny and a continuity of national purpose sublimated political partisanship.[7]

After his triumph in unraveling the Samoan tangle, Secretary Blaine turned to another assignment dearer to his heart. The First International Conference of the American States, which was the direct outgrowth of his earlier call for a Pan-American meeting at the beginning of the decade, convened in Washington, D.C., in October 1889. Blaine was elected president of the proceedings, which attracted delegates from eighteen hemispheric nations, including the United States. The Harrison administration's optimistic agenda included proposals for a *zollvereien*, or customs union, the creation of inter-American rail and steamship lines, an arbitration process to settle disputes among the nations of the hemisphere, copyright and extradition agreements, and a common silver coin. The overall purpose of these proposals was to fulfill Blaine's long-held dream of establishing the United States as the leading political and economic power in the hemisphere and, equally important, to eliminate Great Britain's commercial predominance throughout Latin America.

The maestro was back at work and in prime form, orchestrating public support for his Pan-American project. To help the American conference delegation achieve the ambitious goal of commercial ascendancy in the hemisphere, the secretary of state sent out a circular to boards of trade and chambers of commerce across the nation requesting their views on what was needed to increase the United States'

trade with South America. Blaine also used the occasion of the conference to showcase proudly the United States' prodigious economic
power and advanced industrial technology, which he believed would
serve as an inspiration for Latin Americans in their own quest for mo-
dernity. This blatant boosterism was epitomized in a meticulously
planned and highly publicized cross-country excursion. A day after
their first organizing session, the delegates embarked on a forty-two-
day, six thousand-mile tour of the United States that featured the nation's magnificent cities and bustling industrial centers. Newspapers
throughout the country reported on the progress of the trip and
drummed up support for the conference and the Harrison administration's agenda.

Not all the Latin American delegates were seduced by the glitzy
hype and manipulative publicity. At the outset of the proceedings, the
Argentines were suspicious and wary of the United States' motives
and refused to participate in the promotional tour that highlighted
U.S. industrial might. A Mexican delegate, Matias Romero, in an article published in the prestigious *North American Review,* correctly sur-
mised that the conference was designed "to secure the political and
commercial ascendancy of the United States on this continent." British
observers attacked the purpose of the conference as well, charging
that it was a thinly disguised attempt to "dictate from Washington
the external and even the internal policy of the most important South
American States." Whitelaw Reid, newly appointed minister to France,
reported to his friend Blaine that Europeans were convinced the conference was doing "good work for us," even though they "have had a
great dislike and suspicion of it" from the start. Ultimately, the fears of
the Latin Americans and Europeans were justified. In the first two decades of the twentieth century the United States' prevailing imperial
ideology, coupled with its emerging commercial and political hegemony, led to the practice of gunboat diplomacy and frequent military
interventions to protect American economic interests in the Caribbean
and Central America.[8]

In an effort to avoid just such an undesirable future outcome in
hemispheric relations, the Latin American delegates to the Washington
Pan-American conference introduced a resolution designed to control
and regulate the activities of foreign capitalists in their respective
countries. The resolution stipulated that a sovereign nation "neither
requires nor recognizes any obligations or responsibilities of aliens beyond those established by the Constitution and laws for the native
born in the same conditions." The purpose of this proposal was to prevent foreign investors, in cases of dispute with a host country, from

appealing to their home governments for diplomatic support and possible military intervention, which, the Latin Americans argued, was a direct violation of national sovereignty. Although the United States opposed the resolution and caused its defeat, the North American republic did accept the conference-approved arbitration mechanism to settle legal disputes and possible conflicts among American nations. All the nations in attendance, including the United States, also agreed to oppose any territorial acquisitions by aggression or conquest.

Beyond the arbitration agreement, which was never put into effect because individual governments failed to ratify it, and the self-imposed pledge against territorial aggression, the accomplishments of the First International Conference of the American States were generally disappointing. Argentina blocked the movement for a customs union because it feared the plan would limit its meat and wheat exports to Great Britain and other European customers. Instead of the customs union, the conferees suggested interested countries negotiate separate bilateral reciprocity treaties, a top priority for Harrison and Blaine even before the conference adjourned. On the positive side of the ledger, the conference did set the precedent for future Pan-American meetings and established the International Union of American Republics, which by 1910 had evolved into the Pan-American Union and in 1948 became the present-day Organization of American States. Finally, a March 1890 congressional resolution authorizing President Harrison to invite the Hawaiian kingdom to attend the conference provided a revealing sidenote to the formal proceedings. Although Hawaii's acceptance arrived after the conference ended, the mere fact that Congress took this action highlighted once again that Blaine's blueprints for an American system extending to the mid-Pacific had gained acceptance among a broad spectrum of the nation's leadership. As Blaine pointed out in expressing his regrets to the Hawaiians that the offer had come so late, it was "the peculiar importance of Hawaii as one of the geographical extremes of the American system" that had prompted the tardy invitation in the first place.[9]

Throughout the conference Secretary Blaine did his best to assure its success. Most of the Latin American delegates found him to be objective and fair in his capacity as president, "possessing exquisite tact" and a "desire to prevent the failure of a high purpose." In April 1890, as the conference was winding down, he reported to President Harrison: "I expected to see you this morning but my house was full of Pan-Americans before I was thru breakfast. We are holding two sessions daily—at 11 and at 3." For his part, Harrison later acknowledged that any failure to achieve the administration's goals at the conference did not result from a lack of commitment by the secretary of state. The president justly praised the secretary's efforts, saying that "In the conference of the American Republics Mr. Blaine did a very hard, successful and brilliant work."[10]

Perhaps James G. Blaine's greatest single contribution as secretary of state was his vision of Pan-Americanism and his tenacity in launching the modern Pan-American movement. One too frequently forgotten tribute to the continuing relevance of his hemispheric vision is the splendid and imposing headquarters of the Organization of American States, formerly the Pan-American Union Building, at the corner of Seventeenth Street and Constitution Avenue in the nation's capital. This marvelous building, with an open courtyard and large skylight as its center, was constructed between 1908 and 1910, with $850,000 in seed money from Andrew Carnegie, Blaine's friend and an American delegate to the first conference. The United States government donated the land for the site and the other countries in the hemisphere made individual contributions to complete the project.

It was quite remarkable that Blaine functioned so effectively as a statesman and leader during the Pan-American conference and, for that matter, for the remainder of his tenure as secretary of state until his resignation in 1892. In addition to being weakened physically by his own deteriorating health, he suffered terrible personal loss. Within the span of thirty months, he and his wife unexpectedly lost the three eldest of their six children. At about the midpoint of the conference in January 1890, the eldest child, Walker, died of pneumonia at the age of thirty-four. Fewer than three weeks later, on February 2, 1890, their oldest daughter, Alice Coppinger, died at the age of thirty after a brief illness. Then in June 1892, their second son, Emmons, died in his thirty-fifth year of acute appendicitis. Blaine was particularly close to his sons, especially Walker, who was his trusted confidante and right-hand man at the State Department. These devastating personal losses caused a grief-stricken Blaine, near the end of his own life, to reflect sadly to his friend Murat Halstead, "I could have endured all things if my boys had not died."[11]

Throughout these months of excruciating family tragedy, Secretary Blaine carried on rather admirably. In addition to tending to his State Department duties and conference business, he closely followed the discussion in Congress on the McKinley tariff bill, which was being considered while the Pan-American meeting was in session. After the convention delegates rejected the customs union proposal, Secretary Blaine and President Harrison were convinced that reciprocity treaties offered the most viable way to capture Latin American markets for

American exports throughout the hemisphere. Consequently, Blaine vigorously entered the tariff fray, working hard to convince doubters in Congress, especially Republicans, of the importance of the administration's reciprocity program. In what was the last great political fight of his illustrious career, Blaine launched an extensive educational campaign that won over a skeptical William McKinley and led to the inclusion of a reciprocity amendment in the tariff legislation that Congress passed in September 1890. In the final stages of this struggle over the McKinley Tariff Act, while Blaine was recuperating from an illness at his summer cottage in Bar Harbor, Maine, President Harrison's lobbying effort among wavering senators was crucial to the ultimate success of the administration's reciprocity crusade. The two veteran politicians proved a very effective team in pursuit of an economic expansionist tactic that retained protectionism and used reciprocity treaties to enlarge foreign markets.

In their arguments to Congress for approval of reciprocity, the Harrison administration revealed a complementary domestic political goal. The rumblings of agrarian unrest from the prairies were threatening the Republican party's supremacy in several key Midwestern and Western states. The opening of foreign markets through the tactic of reciprocity, reasoned Harrison and Blaine, would calm discontented farmers and overcome the increasingly powerful appeal of the Populist party. Equally important, by opening new trade outlets, the reciprocity policy would dampen the social unrest caused by the recurrent depressions of the late nineteenth century. During the Republican congressional election campaign of 1890, Secretary Blaine made this strategy clear when he spoke to a crowd of five thousand in Waterville, Maine, in late August. One of the "highest duties" of the United States, proclaimed Blaine, was "to enlarge the area of its foreign trade." It would not do to remain satisfied with the home market, "nor would it be an ambitious destiny for so great a country as ours to manufacture only what we can consume, or to produce only what we can eat." At the heart of Blaine's ideology was the belief that economic expansion abroad would provide prosperity at home, which, in turn, would ameliorate domestic social unrest and quell labor and farmer uprisings. "Annexation of trade," he assured his Maine audience, was much preferred to the "annexation of territory." In truth, he wanted both.[12]

The reciprocity program neither ended depression and domestic upheaval nor provided victory for the Republicans at the polls. The GOP was severely defeated in the 1890 congressional elections, and in 1892 Harrison lost the presidency in a rematch with Grover Cleveland.

The eight reciprocity treaties negotiated by the Harrison administration in Central and South America were too short-lived to establish American hegemony in the hemisphere or to overcome the recurrent economic and social difficulties of depression. In the short run, Blaine and Harrison may have oversold the benefits of reciprocity. But in the long run, both for the future success of the Republican party and Blaine's imperial blueprints, the policy of reciprocity remained important. In 1896 William McKinley won the presidential election by skillfully employing the promise of reciprocity as one important plank in his successful campaign platform. In Hawaii, reciprocity had tied that island kingdom politically and economically to the United States and served as a backdrop to a revolution in 1893 that overthrew the monarchy. It also put the lie to Blaine's claim that the United States was no longer interested in the annexation of territory.

The diplomatic pressure on the Hawaiian kingdom to bind itself irrevocably to the United States began in the opening weeks of the Harrison administration. Fearing that Hawaiian sugar growers were in danger of losing special access to the American market, Hawaii's minister to Washington, Henry A. P. Carter, met almost immediately with the newly installed secretary of state. Blaine, for his part, was intent on more tightly securing American rights to Pearl Harbor, and he apparently suggested to Carter that they proceed to negotiate a treaty that would establish Hawaii as a protectorate of the United States. On April 11, 1889, Minister Carter submitted a proposal to Blaine that provided for complete trade reciprocity between the Hawaiian Islands and the United States. In addition, Washington was to promise to guarantee the independence and autonomy of Hawaii. To allow the United States to fulfill this guarantee of independence, the Hawaiian monarch agreed not to enter into treaties with other foreign nations without the formal consent of the U.S. government. The final provision of the proposed treaty made clear the full nature of the protectorate: it allowed the United States to use armed force to preserve domestic peace and protect and preserve Hawaiian sovereignty from foreign threat.

Back in Honolulu, King Kalakaua and his cabinet balked at the provisions of the Carter-Blaine agreement, especially the proviso for landing troops on Hawaiian soil. After several months of deliberation with his advisors, the Hawaiian monarch suggested a revision to the treaty. The Hawaiians would accept the provision to seek approval from the United States before negotiating a treaty with another nation, but they removed the article that allowed the American government to intervene militarily in the affairs of the island kingdom. However, King Kalakaua, who had twice visited the United States and had met Secretary Blaine during his first trip in the 1870s when the Maine Republican was speaker of the House, remained wary of the Harrison administration's intentions and feared the Americans sought to undermine Hawaii's independence. Kalakaua refused to send instructions to Minister Carter to seek the necessary revisions in the proposed treaty, and by the spring of 1890 the scheme for a protectorate appeared dead.

The next move in this high stakes diplomatic poker game came from the United States. The McKinley tariff bill, which was being debated and revised during the spring and summer of 1890, placed sugar on the free list. This meant that Hawaiian sugar growers lost the major benefit derived from the renewed 1887 reciprocity treaty that ceded Pearl Harbor to the United States. The Hawaiian government protested this change and asked the Harrison administration to restore Hawaii's favored position and do justice to the previous reciprocity agreements. Secretary Blaine apparently gave the Hawaiian minister the impression that justice would be done, but when the final version of the McKinley tariff legislation was approved, there was no provision for a special status for Hawaiian goods. The omission of an exemption may have been a clerical error, as claimed by the American government. The oversight was corrected by Congress in March 1891, although the free sugar provision remained. From the Hawaiian monarchy's perspective, however, it appeared that Blaine and Harrison deliberately were applying economic pressure on the kingdom in an attempt to get the protectorate they sought or better yet, to annex the islands.

Early on in the struggle over the treaty, the British government learned of the Harrison administration's intentions. Concerned that the treaty threatened British interests in the Hawaiian Islands, Sir Julian Pauncefote, Britain's minister to Washington, suggested to Secretary Blaine that their two nations reiterate their commitment, originally expressed unilaterally by the two nations in the 1840s, to guarantee Hawaii's independence. "Mr. Blaine," Pauncefote reported, "in a very emphatic way said the United States would do nothing of the kind." Later, after the protectorate scheme collapsed, Blaine privately wrote to Harrison about future territorial acquisitions: "I think there are only three places that are of value enough to be taken, that are not continental. One is Hawaii and the others are Cuba and Porto Rico. Cuba and Porto Rico are not now imminent and will not be for a generation. Hawaii may come up for decision at an unexpected hour and I hope we shall be prepared to decide it in the affirmative." Rather than the establishment of a mere protectorate, the ultimate goal of the Harrison administration appeared to have become the formal annexation of Hawaii.[13]

In 1889 Secretary of State James G. Blaine appointed his old friend, John L. Stevens, as minister to Hawaii. Stevens was a faithful ally and like-minded expansionist, who at a spry sixty-nine still could be counted on to carry out the Harrison administration's imperial designs in that far-off chain of islands at the crossroads of the Pacific Ocean. Blaine and Stevens had begun their careers together thirty-five years earlier as partners and editors of the *Kennebec Journal* in Augusta. Luther Severance, the just-returned American commissioner to the Sandwich Islands and former editor of the newspaper, had tutored these fledgling journalists on Hawaii's importance to America's destiny in the Pacific Rim. Both men had absorbed Severance's fascination with those islands, and from 1854 to 1855 they had written several editorials advocating the annexation of Hawaii. Throughout their lengthy public careers, Blaine and Stevens remained committed to bringing that island kingdom into the "American system." In sending John L. Stevens to Hawaii on what would be his last diplomatic assignment, Secretary Blaine trusted his old comrade would make his best effort to realize finally their mutually shared dream.

Minister Stevens arrived in Honolulu in the summer of 1889 without the benefit of written instructions officially defining his mission. His subsequent actions over the next three and one-half years, culminating in his decision to land American marines in support of a coup that overthrew the Hawaiian monarchy in January 1893, remain controversial to the present day. The issue then, as now, was whether or not Stevens was acting independently and without the approval of Washington, or whether he had received a carte blanche directive from Secretary Blaine to support whatever action necessary to bring about American annexation of the islands. In 1993, a century after the Hawaiian revolution, the United States, in a joint resolution passed by the House and Senate and signed into law by President Bill Clinton, commemorated the one hundredth anniversary of the coup that toppled Queen Liliuokalani. Commonly known as the "Apology Bill," the legislation skirted the issue of responsibility and simply extended a formal apology to native Hawaiians "on behalf of the United States for the overthrow of the Kingdom of Hawaii." That same year, prior to the passage of the Apology Bill, the United Church of Christ, which began sending missionaries to Hawaii in 1820 through its American Board of

Commissioners for Foreign Missions, also apologized to the native Hawaiian people in candid recognition of the complicity of some of its church members in the 1893 overthrow of the Hawaiian monarchy.[14]

What prompted these official expressions of regret and remorse from the president, the Congress, and the synod of the United Church of Christ? Why the calls for reconciliation with the native Hawaiians from legislators and religious leaders a century after the event? Undoubtedly, in both cases the primary motivation was one of honor and justice generated by a sense of guilt about a past imperial wrong and the need to acknowledge the mistake by offering native Hawaiians a formal apology. In addition, these actions were a direct political response to the resurgence of Hawaiian nationalism that surfaced in the 1970s and 1980s. This "Hawaiian Renaissance" encouraged pride in Hawaiian culture, language, and traditions and publicized past events that, for many residents of the state of Hawaii, were an unknown history of the Hawaiian nation and its monarchy. Some Hawaiian nationalists merely sought an apology from the U.S. government for its role in the coup, but others demanded reparations and the return of communal lands. However, the 1993 apology legislation, or Public Law 103-150, did not acknowledge the native Hawaiian demands for compensation or reparations because there was no proof of the intent or malice of the American government, as represented by Secretary of State Blaine and President Harrison. The implied conclusion of the Apology Bill was that Minister John L. Stevens had acted on his own authority, without formal approval from Washington.[15]

While no evidence has surfaced that proves Minister Stevens received an official "smoking gun" directive to support whatever action necessary, including a coup against the Queen, to guarantee American annexation of the islands, there certainly was an unspoken complicity—in this case, silence *was* consent—coupled with an unmistakable unity of purpose on the part of key members of the Harrison administration. Stevens sent a number of dispatches to Blaine and his successor at the State Department, John W. Foster, in the period 1890–1892, asking for advice on what course to follow in Hawaii. Revolutionary activity was brewing in the islands because of dissatisfaction with the economic downturn caused by the McKinley tariff, and the American minister believed "annexation must be the future remedy" to prevent the islands from becoming a "possession of Great Britain." What should the U.S. minister and the naval commander do if there was a surprise overturn of the Hawaiian monarchy? Stevens believed Hawaii was at a turning point and must choose between the path to Asia or that which "binds her to the care of American destiny." What action did the secretary of state favor? "I want you," Stevens finally asked Blaine in March 1892, "to write me in as few or many words as you please—are you for Annexation?"[16]

Secretary Blaine responded to Minister Stevens' alarmist queries in a most formal and perfunctory manner. He did not say the administration favored annexation nor did the secretary of state tell his man in Honolulu what action to take if a revolution against the monarchy erupted. He was silent on these issues, adhering to the dictum frequently invoked by twentieth-century policymakers: if it is really important, do not put it in writing. The fact that the secretary of state did not write to Stevens saying he disapproved of providing American diplomatic or military support for a revolt against the established government of Queen Liliuokalani confirmed for his old friend that Washington tacitly approved his actions and his fervor for annexation. Blaine had numerous opportunities to rein in Stevens if he chose, but he did not. Minister Stevens was justified in thinking his superior's silence was consent. In addition, the correspondence between Blaine and Harrison in these crucial months revealed their approval of Stevens' line of thought. In October 1891, Harrison wrote to his secretary of state about a recent note received from Stevens, concluding that "the necessity of maintaining and increasing our hold and influence in the Sandwich Islands is very apparent and very pressing."[17]

In early 1892 a small group of leaders of American background formed a secret organization in Hawaii called the Annexation Club. This group was led by Lorrin A. Thurston, a dynamic lawyer and ardent promoter of annexation, who schemed with Minister Stevens to bring the Hawaiian Islands into the American union. Thurston journeyed to the mainland that spring, ostensibly to plan for Hawaii's exhibit at the upcoming Chicago World's Columbian Exposition of 1893, a celebration of the four hundredth anniversary of Christopher Columbus's arrival in the new world. After finishing his business in Chicago, Thurston went to Washington as an agent of the Annexation Club. He had a letter of introduction from Minister John L. Stevens and met with several congressional leaders, one of whom he reportedly told: "I mean to endeavor to bring about the annexation of the islands." Thurston next met with Secretary of State Blaine and informed him of the political unrest in Hawaii and dissatisfaction with the Queen's rule. Blaine was seriously ill at the time and would resign from the State Department on June 4, 1892, a few weeks after his interview with the undercover agent of the Annexation Club. At their meeting Blaine gave a "green light" to Thurston, who later recounted that the secretary of state assured him that "if the people of the Islands applied to the United States for annexation, he did not see how the application could be rejected."[18]

In light of all this evidence of Blaine's and the Harrison administration's support for Hawaiian annexation, it is difficult to accept the view that Minister John L. Stevens was merely a "rogue elephant," acting without authorization from his government. His decision to send the marines ashore in January 1893, in support of the coup led by the Thurston group was consistent with the wishes of his superiors. Stevens had no fear of reprisal and none was forthcoming from the Harrison administration. When a treaty of annexation was negotiated with the new provisional government, President Harrison promptly submitted it to the Senate for approval. At the time, Stevens enthusiastically wrote the State Department: "The Hawaiian pear is now fully ripe, and this is the golden hour for the United States to pluck it." The incoming president, Democrat Grover Cleveland, who had defeated Harrison in the 1892 election, reversed this policy and did not pluck the pear. Instead, he relieved Stevens of his post and withdrew the annexation treaty from the Senate. Hawaii was not to be annexed until 1898 during the Spanish-American War when another Republican, William McKinley, sat in the executive mansion.[19]

During his tenure as minister to the Hawaiian Islands, John L. Stevens also confirmed the role missionaries played in bringing those Pacific islands into the American imperial orbit. His analysis of the importance of those nonstate actors to American overseas expansion was more comprehensive and more accurate than that offered by the Church of Christ in its 1993 apology to the native Hawaiians. As students of Luther Severance in the 1850s, Stevens and Blaine had come to understand the role of missionaries as agents of empire in Hawaii. This awareness was best expressed by Stevens when he wrote to Blaine from Honolulu that, "For more than half a century the American Missionary Board with the agencies and influence in its control, has served as a strong fortress to the United States in these islands. The large financial contributions, amounting to nearly one million dollars, which that organization obtained through innumerable channels of American benevolence and religious zeal, and the large number of educated and resolute agents which it sent to these islands, secured an influence over the ruling chiefs and native population which held them as firmly as a permanent military force could have done." Minister Stevens clarified what Blaine already knew: volunteerism and private financing, as well as governmental support, were crucial to the expansion of American influence abroad. Throughout the nineteenth century, it was nonstate actors—not only individual missionaries in the field but also the faithful at home—who were doing the work of empire.[20]

In the Caribbean, as in Hawaii, Secretary Blaine was willing to use revolution and internal disorder to promote his imperial agenda. Blaine tried to coerce the dominant faction struggling for control of Haiti into granting the United States a naval station and allowing it to represent Haitian diplomatic interests in the capitals of Europe. When his request was denied, the secretary of state directly influenced the outcome of the internal revolution by ignoring an existing blockade and allowing American goods to supply the opposition faction. The Haitian opposition leader, Hyppolite, ultimately triumphed over his rival and established control over the nation. Because they helped Hyppolite by lifting the blockade, Secretary Blaine and President Harrison assumed the new government would be more amenable to the United States' request for a naval base in Haiti.

The formal task of securing an American naval station on Haiti's northwestern coast at Mole St. Nicolas, a harbor that lies approximately one hundred miles and virtually due east across the Windward Passage from the present-day American naval base at Guantánamo, Cuba, was assigned to Frederick Douglass. In 1889 the Harrison administration appointed the prominent African-American leader and Republican party loyalist as minister to Haiti with instructions to seek concessions, including a coaling station, from the new regime. It should be remembered that Douglass, unlike Secretary Blaine, had long supported American expansion in the Caribbean, and during the Grant administration—when Blaine as speaker of the House had opposed the scheme—"was for the acquisition of Samana, and of Santo Domingo herself if she wished to come to us." When, after a year of haggling, the negotiations for concessions proved fruitless, Blaine grew impatient and, in a move strongly resented by Minister Douglass, sent a white naval officer, Rear Admiral Bancroft Gerhardi, with special instructions to secure a lease for a naval base at Mole St. Nicolas. Again, the Haitians resisted the American overtures. Blaine next attempted to intimidate the recalcitrant Haitians with a show of naval force in the waters surrounding their capital city, Port-au-Prince. All to no avail, as Haiti once more firmly refused to grant the United States a naval station on its territory.[21]

After their disappointment in Haiti, Blaine and Harrison focused their attention on acquiring a naval base in the Dominican Republic. In June 1891 the administration negotiated a reciprocity treaty with the Dominican Republic and pressed as well for a lease of Samana Bay, a port coveted by the United States since the days of Seward and Grant. After months of secret talks with the Dominican government, Blaine and Harrison had no better luck than previous administrations in securing an agreement for Samana Bay, and they subsequently abandoned their quest for a naval facility in the Caribbean. Nonetheless, Blaine remained sanguine about the future. The secretary of state confidently assumed, as he confided to President Harrison, that the two far more strategically important islands, Cuba and Puerto Rico, were destined to come under American control within a generation or so. He correctly anticipated that the Caribbean would became an American lake and serve as the strategic safeguard for a projected American-controlled isthmian canal. But Blaine's patience and seeming restraint in the Caribbean masked the fact that his imperial blueprints had undergone a final alteration. Support for revolutions and the use of economic and diplomatic coercion, possibly even military intervention, whether in Hawaii or Haiti, were now seen as viable tactics for the United States to employ in its drive for overseas territorial expansion.

The Harrison administration may have stopped short of using military force in Haiti, but on at least one occasion President Harrison appeared quite willing to employ force against another nation. In 1891–1892 a crisis with Chile erupted over a fracas in Valparaiso between the crew of the American ship, *Baltimore,* and a Chilean mob. Two American sailors were killed and a number were injured. The Chilean government dragged its feet and did not offer either an apology or reparations. An enraged Harrison threatened military intervention and brought the United States to the brink of war to avenge what he deemed an unpardonable insult to American honor. Harrison's bellicose stance nearly undermined Blaine's Pan-American project and the administration's painstaking effort to foster better relations among the nations of the hemisphere.

Chilean animosity toward the United States extended back for at least a decade and, to a marked degree, focused on the activities and official statements of James G. Blaine. Blaine had aroused Chilean ire when, as secretary of state under Garfield, he gave his diplomatic support to Peru in the War of the Pacific and leveled charges that Chile's military adventure had been inspired by Great Britain. In addition, Chileans were stung by Blaine's denunciation of the growing British control of their nation's nitrate industry. The increasingly dominant role British capital played in their economy undoubtedly worried Chilean nationalists, but they also resented Blaine's meddling in their affairs. When he returned to the State Department in 1889, Blaine was pleased to discover that the Chilean political landscape had changed and that the ruling government of José Manuel Balmaceda was intent on curtailing British influence in Chile. To take advantage of this new opportunity to undermine British economic predominance on the Pacific coast of South America, Secretary Blaine appointed Patrick Egan as American minister to Santiago. Egan, an Irish patriot who had emigrated to the United States in the early 1880s, was an implacable foe of Great Britain. As a believer in Blaine's agenda for overseas economic expansion, Minister Egan was sympathetic to Balmaceda's campaign to preserve "Chile for Chileans."

Whatever hope Egan and Blaine had for extending American political and commercial interests in Chile faded in early 1891 when that nation plunged into civil war. The defeat of Balmaceda was a bitter setback for Harrison's and Blaine's ambitions along the Pacific rim of South America. President Harrison was particularly embittered, which partially explains why he responded so vehemently to the *Baltimore* incident and the new government's tardiness in offering an apology and monetary compensation. Blaine was sick much of the time during crucial stages in the crisis with Chile, and Harrison was carrying much of the diplomatic load. The president became impatient and increasingly bellicose and by early January 1892, appeared ready to go to war with Chile. Blaine tried to rein in Harrison, urging caution and restraint. Although the secretary of state advised against sending an ultimatum to Chile, he did so at the insistence of the president. As Henry Cabot Lodge reported after a dinner with Harrison and the secretary of state, Blaine was "all for peace." It was President Harrison who pressed forward for war, and his apparent willingness to use military force bullied the new Chilean government into issuing an apology and accepting American demands. Even then, Blaine and Republican leaders in Congress had to press Harrison to back off and accept Chile's apology.[22]

For his judicious handling of the Chilean crisis as well as for his general management of the State Department during his second tenure as secretary, Blaine earned the accolades of his colleagues and won the grudging respect of some of his enemies. No longer routinely and pejoratively dismissed as Jingo Jim, Blaine had achieved a certain stature as a statesman who was deemed worthy of being mentioned in the same breath, as Harrison had years earlier, with Germany's Otto von Bismarck and British leaders such as William E. Gladstone and the marquis of Salisbury. He appeared to have bested Bismarck over Samoa and requited himself well when tangling with Lord Salisbury during a controversy with Great Britain over the Canadian practice of killing fur-bearing seals in the Bering Sea. Blaine took the high ground in this dispute by expounding the environmentally sensitive position that the hunting of seals in the open seas, known as pelagic sealing, placed the entire Bering Sea seal population in jeopardy and violated international morality, or, in the diplomatic terminology of the time, was *contra bonos mores*. Although the final arbitrated settlement of the dispute was reached after the Harrison administration left office and was unfavorable to the United States on all counts, Secretary Blaine should be credited for his farsighted diplomacy. His position was upheld when the arbitration award placed restrictions on pelagic sealing and instituted conservation measures that protected the seal population of the Bering Sea.

The relationship between Secretary Blaine and President Harrison became increasingly tense toward the end of the negotiations that led to the agreement for arbitration of the Bering Sea controversy. Harrison undoubtedly was a bit testy and resentful about the workload he had to carry because of Blaine's incapacitating illnesses and poor health. Perhaps he was irked as well by the condescending tone of some of Blaine's correspondence. For instance, in a March 1892 memorandum that Blaine was too sick to sign, the secretary of state revealed he was troubled by his chief's diplomacy and lectured him about the folly of trying to "get up a war cry" and sending naval ships to the Bering Sea. President Harrison also was suspicious that the ever-popular Plumed Knight was scheming to deny him renomination and that Blaine hoped to be the GOP candidate that year. Harrison's fears about James G. Blaine's presidential ambitions were unwarranted. Blaine was much too ill and frail to stage another campaign for the nation's highest office. Indeed, the secretary of state knew he was dying. Earlier, Blaine privately had explained to Nelson Dingley, a fellow Republican from Maine, that "my preference is to remain in the cabinet. My work as Secretary of State was sadly interrupted by the death of President Garfield. The country never fully understood my policy. I desire to complete the work I have now undertaken. I do not feel that my health will admit of my going thru another presidential campaign."[23]

Secretary of State Blaine resigned on June 4, 1892. President Harrison, ever distrustful of his friend and rival, questioned the timing of Blaine's departure, suspecting that the secretary was leaving the State Department to prepare his bid for the party's nomination at the upcoming Republican national convention. The paranoid Harrison was mistaken, as he easily won renomination on the first ballot. In November, however, he was soundly defeated in his rematch with Grover Cleveland. Blaine, once again devastated by family tragedy when his son Emmons died suddenly a few days after the Republican convention adjourned, gave only one speech in Harrison's behalf during the fall campaign. In an elaborately planned reception for him at the Westchester county home of Whitelaw Reid, who was the Republican vice presidential candidate, Blaine spoke to an assembled crowd of three thousand, extolling the virtues of the protective tariff as the source of the nation's prosperity and economic progress. In a follow-up speech laced with anti-British barbs that delighted the audience, Chauncey Depew hailed James G. Blaine as "an American of Americans," and the "one foreign minister who has commanded the respect and fear of the whole world." Depew's remarks served as a fitting political eulogy for the statesman and politician who had been Mr. Republican for more than a decade.[24]

Even in retirement, wracked by grief and pain and with but six months to live, Blaine's unbridled optimism about the nation's destiny shone through. In anticipation of the 1893 Chicago's World Columbian Exposition, he contributed an essay entitled "The Progress and Development of the Western World" for an illustrated volume, *Columbus and Columbia*. Dedicated to national unity and American patriotism, the book was another attempt, more than a quarter of a century after the conflict ended, to heal the wounds of the Civil War and bury "the bloody shirt." The reverse side of the volume's title page featured an illustration depicting a Union soldier clasping the hand of a Confederate soldier in friendship and mutual respect. Not surprisingly, the theme of Blaine's article was that the late nineteenth-century United States represented the culmination of Western progress and that its destiny was to foster human liberty and economic progress and be the wellspring of democracy. "The America of today," Blaine proclaimed, "belongs to Americans." Its responsibility to the human race was both to meet the challenges and opportunities of "continental empire" and to carry forth the hope and promise of western civilization.[25]

When James G. Blaine died on January 27, 1893, there was an immense outpouring of national grief. He was hailed across the length and breadth of the land as an American leader and statesman of the first rank. The *Chicago Tribune's* praise of Blaine's "imperial statesmanship" was typical of that expressed throughout the nation's press. The editors linked his death to the revolution that had occurred in Hawaii ten days earlier: "He was in favor of the annexation of Hawaii, not so much for the smaller reasons that for half a century it has been under American influences, not because 90 per cent of its trade is controlled by this country, not because the property of the American residents are so great, but for the greater reason that its possession meant supremacy over the commerce of the Pacific, and removed forever the fear that the United States would be cooped up within its present limits." The Chicago newspaper also approvingly quoted Blaine, claiming that "some four years ago," he had clarified the key features of his imperial blueprints for the American public: "With control of the Nicaraguan Canal, with Hawaii annexed, and with a coaling station on the island of Santo Domingo, we should be absolute mistress of the American continent and of the waters thereabout. With this done there is no scheme of territorial or commercial conquest that we could not work to success." Whether or not this statement was apocryphal, it accurately sketched out the expansionist agenda Blaine pursued during his years as secretary of state in the Harrison administration.[26]

James G. Blaine's imperial blueprints had originally been drafted when he was a newspaper editor in Maine. As a congressman and senator, he revised and modified these plans always with one goal uppermost in his mind: he wanted the United States to fulfill its national destiny by achieving economic and political hegemony in the Western Hemisphere and the Pacific Rim. Blaine's imperial blueprints went through their final revisions in the last years of his life. More than twenty years before, in the early 1870s, when the Grant administration favored taking control of Caribbean bases and territory, Speaker Blaine had opposed that imperial course of action. By the time of his second tenure as secretary of state, he had changed his mind and come to favor taking direct control of territorial possessions overseas. This was true for Hawaii in his own lifetime, and he anticipated it would be true for the next generation in the Caribbean islands, such as Cuba and Puerto Rico. As it turned out, all three territories would become integral parts of an overseas American empire within six years after his death.

Notes

1. Robert L. Beisner, *From the Old Diplomacy to the New, 1865–1900* (Arlington Heights, IL: Harlan Davidson, Inc., 1986), 97; Benjamin Harrison to James G. Blaine, January 17, 1889; Blaine to Harrison, January 21, 1889, in *The Correspondence Between Benjamin Harrison and James G. Blaine, 1882–1893,* ed. Albert T. Volwiler (Philadelphia: American Philosophical Society, 1940), 44–50.

2. Quoted in Nathan Miller, *Theodore Roosevelt, A Life* (New York: William Morrow and Company, 1992), 203.

3. Harrison to Whitelaw Reid, October 21, 1891, Whitelaw Reid Papers, Library of Congress.

4. Fred Harvey Harrington, *God, Mammon and the Japanese: Dr. Horace Allen*

and Korean-American Relations, 1884–1905 (Madison: University of Wisconsin Press, 1966), 135.

5. Blaine to John A. Kasson, William W. Phelps, and George H. Bates, April 11, 1889, *Foreign Relations of the United States, 1889* (Washington, DC: Government Printing Office, 1890), 201.

6. Blaine to Mrs. Anna Lodge, quoted in John A. S. Grenville and George Berkeley Young, *Politics, Strategy, and American Diplomacy* (New Haven: Yale University Press, 1966), 217.

7. Foster Rhea Dulles, *America in the Pacific: A Century of Expansion* (Boston: Houghton Mifflin Company, 1932), 124.

8. Matias Romero, "The Pan American Conference," *North American Review* 151 (1890), 436; *London Times,* July 15, 1890.

9. Alice Felt Tyler, *The Foreign Policy of James G. Blaine* (Hamden, CT: Archon Books, 1965), 183.

10. Blaine to Harrison, April 15, 1890; Harrison memoranda on his relations with Blaine, May 22, 1893, in Volwiler, *Correspondence,* 100, 302.

11. Murat Halstead, "The Defeat of Blaine for the Presidency," *McClure's Magazine,* January 1896, 172.

12. *New York Tribune,* August 30, 1890.

13. Julian Pauncefote to the Marquis of Salisbury, January 10, 1890, quoted in Walter LaFeber, *The American Search for Opportunity, 1865–1913* (New York: Cambridge University Press, 1993), 93; Blaine to Harrison, August 10, 1891, in Volwiler, *Correspondence,* 174.

14. *U.S. Statutes at Large* 107 (1993): 1510–14.

15. Alan Murakami, "The Apology Bill: 'What Is It Good for?'" *Ka Wai Ola o OHA,* Office of Hawaiian Affairs (August 1998), 23.

16. Cited in Charles S. Campbell, *The Transformation of American Foreign Relations, 1865–1900* (New York: Harper and Row, 1976), 180.

17. Harrison to Blaine, October 14, 1891, in Volwiler, *Correspondence,* 206.

18. Cited in Julius W. Pratt, *Expansionists of 1898* (Baltimore: Johns Hopkins Press, 1936), 56.

19. Ibid., *Expansionists,* 113.

20. John L. Stevens to Blaine, March 20, 1890, quoted in Richard C. Winchester, "James G. Blaine and the Ideology of American Expansionism," (Ph.D. diss., University of Rochester, 1966), 178.

21. Frederick Douglass, "Haiti and the United States," *North American Review* 153 (1891): 340.

22. John A. Garraty, *Henry Cabot Lodge, A Biography* (New York: Alfred A. Knopf, 1953), 149.

23. Quoted in Edward Nelson Dingley, *The Life and Times of Nelson Dingley, Jr.* (Kalamazoo, MI: Ihling Bros. and Everard, 1902), 344.

24. Quoted in David S. Muzzey, *James G. Blaine: A Political Idol of Other Days* (New York: Dodd, Mead and Company, 1935), 482.

25. James G. Blaine, "The Progress and Development of the Western World," in *Columbus and Columbia* (Richmond, VA: B. F. Johnson and Co., 1892), 57.

26. *Chicago Tribune,* January 31, 1893.

Imperial Legacies

It will be Mr. Blaine's strongest title to a great place in our history that he was the American statesman of the last quarter of the nineteenth century who most fully perceived the part that his country must play in the Twentieth.
—*Review of Reviews*, March 1893

Secretary Blaine would be satisfied with his handiwork if he could today see the outgrowth of the policies which he upheld and of the plans which he initiated.
—Sumner Welles, January 27, 1943

James G. Blaine was a man of vision and imagination. He began his illustrious career as a teacher and, while still in his twenties, moved on to become a highly successful journalist and newspaper editor. He helped organize the Republican party in Maine, and he initially entered public life as a representative to the state legislature. During the Civil War, Blaine was elected as a representative to Congress and became speaker of the House of Representatives before he was forty years old. He next served in the Senate and twice as secretary of state. Four consecutive times the leading presidential choice of the rank and file of the Republican party, Blaine was the outstanding politician and statesman in American public life for more than a quarter of a century. As a scholarly writer and innovative thinker, he was instrumental in drawing up the plans and laying the intellectual and ideological groundwork for America's late nineteenth-century overseas commercial and territorial expansion. Among his peers, James G. Blaine was the acknowledged architect of American empire and national greatness. He was, for his generation of Americans, the gifted and able planner who served as a key transitional figure in American diplomacy, linking the foreign policy of the antebellum period to the burst of imperialism at the turn of the century.

As a visionary and farsighted statesman, James G.

Blaine was, as one of his many pupils, Elihu Root, noted, a leader "in advance of his time." From the beginning, Blaine fashioned his imperial vision into blueprints for energetic governmental action in support of overseas economic expansion that included federal aid for a revitalized merchant marine, the building of a first-class navy, and the acquisition of naval stations in the Caribbean and the Pacific to protect the nation's growing foreign trade. He also envisioned unilateral American control of a projected isthmian canal and the creation of the United States' political and commercial hegemony in the Western Hemisphere. In pursuit of these ambitious goals, Blaine of Maine, the famed Plumed Knight to legions of his rabid followers, and Jingo Jim to his enemies and detractors, became a symbol of the new aggressiveness of American diplomacy in the 1880s and 1890s and was identified as a leading proponent of the republic's glorious national destiny and future greatness. Quite simply, it was James G. Blaine who prepared his fellow citizens for the upcoming American century.

Another bedrock in the foundation of Blaine's imperial vision was his strongly held belief that Great Britain presented the main obstacle to the United States' global ambitions. Blaine's early mentors, Henry Clay and John Quincy Adams, had by their example instructed him in the threat posed by British power and imperial sway. Throughout his political and diplomatic career, Blaine harbored an abiding distrust and resentment of Great Britain and the British establishment. An Anglophobe, he relished twisting the British lion's tail, and a visceral anti-British nationalism was a basic feature of his global outlook. Obsessed with removing Britain as the leading economic power in the Western Hemisphere, Blaine fathered a policy of Pan-Americanism designed to challenge and overcome British commercial supremacy in Central and South America. That would be the first phase in what Blaine described as "the race for development and empire." Ultimately, he sought to displace an imperially preeminent Great Britain by winning global economic supremacy for the United States and transforming the American republic into the world's number one power.

Despite this hostility for Britain as the nation's chief rival in the competition for world economic supremacy, Blaine admired British traditions, institutions, and culture, and he linked Anglo-Saxonism with an American sense of mission. He took pride in the nation's British heritage and expected the United States to carry on the Anglo-Saxon legacy. For someone as publicly anti-British as James G. Blaine, equating American national greatness and mission with Anglo-Saxonism appeared to be a contradiction in terms. But Blaine was untroubled by this lack of consistency. He believed, as did most British leaders, in a racial hierarchy in which Anglo-Saxons were at the top of the scale. Blaine and his generation of Americans also shared with their British cousins a set of cultural perceptions, which, along with race, included similar Victorian attitudes toward religion and gender. In addition, Blaine believed that several innate traits, biologically determined as well as culturally acquired, characterized the economic and political success of English-speaking peoples. Among these were superior intelligence, industry, a genius for self-government, and a love of adventure and risk-taking. As he had made clear in one of his last published essays, Blaine saw the United States as the logical inheritor of these traditions and believed its future destiny was to preserve human liberty and promote economic progress.

An ardent nationalist and American patriot, James G. Blaine demanded international respect for his nation and its citizens. His patriotism may have bordered on chauvinism at times, but it would be inaccurate to cast him as an isolationist, narrow-minded, provincial politician who knew nothing of the outside world. Blaine was a well-educated and cosmopolitan leader who twice made the grand tour of Europe. His family was worldly wise as well, and the father made sure his children, especially the sons, received first-rate schooling, including study abroad. As a youth and continuing throughout his adult life, Blaine read widely, treasured good books, and appreciated art, literature, and history, especially that of the British Isles and the United States. On the campaign trail the Plumed Knight's speeches were laced with historical and literary references. He would have been incredulous at a later generation's dismissive contention that the United States was an "isolationist" nation during his lifetime of public service as "a far-seeing statesman," and he would have scoffed at the suggestion that, during his watch, the great American republic was unmindful of its international responsibilities and growing world role.

The ignorance of later generations of Americans about the extent of their nation's global involvement in the 1880s and 1890s partially arose from the fact that the main architect of empire looked south to Latin America and west to the Pacific and Asia. The predominant Eurocentric outlook of most Americans led them to ignore expansion elsewhere. Certainly, Latin Americans, Hawaiians, Samoans, Japanese, Koreans, and Chinese would find it difficult to accept the idea that the United States was an isolationist nation in the nineteenth century. In his campaign to promote overseas commercial and territorial expansion to the south and west, Secretary Blaine devised an "American system." This system relied on the use of the Monroe Doctrine from the Caribbean to all of South America, and in the 1880s Blaine extended its coverage to the Hawaiian Islands, the crossroads of the Pacific Ocean. Blaine primarily viewed the 1823 declaration as shielding hemispheric nations and Pacific kingdoms from European predators, thus safeguarding his American system. But he also interpreted the doctrine in a paternalistic fashion. In his mind, it was a vehicle for American intervention. The United States had an imperial duty to discipline unruly Latin Americans through what Blaine euphemistically dubbed "humane" interventions. A quarter of a century later, President Theodore Roosevelt built upon Blaine's precedent in the Roosevelt Corollary to the Monroe Doctrine, which premised American military intervention on the need to correct "chronic wrongdoing" among the nations of Latin America.

Blaine also effectively used the economic lever of reciprocity treaties to build an American system. The tactic of reciprocity had several advantages. It provided an imaginative way, as the Maine Republican frequently reminded his fellow Americans, to open additional markets for a variety of agricultural and manufactured products without endangering the principle of protectionism at home. Reciprocity also offered a means to level the commercial playing field, especially in Latin America, by negating the trade benefits Britain's transportation and credit facilities provided its exporters and entrepreneurs. The most successful use of the reciprocity tactic came in Hawaii, where the 1875 treaty, renewed in 1887 with a proviso for a naval station at Pearl Harbor, tied that island kingdom to the United States with economic and political hoops of steel. As an expansionist tactic, the policy of reciprocity was the fulcrum in a global strategy upon which hinged future American political and commercial preeminence in the Western Hemisphere and the Pacific basin.

Blaine's carefully assembled portfolio of imperial blueprints went through a series of modifications and refinements. The most notable and telling change was prompted by the question of overseas territorial expansion. Throughout most of his public career, Blaine opposed a formal colonial empire on the British model. He was an informal empire man, who desired the annexation of trade, not territory. But there always had been a loophole in his opposition to grabbing insular possessions and far-off colonies. Blaine believed annexing additional territory would be acceptable "should it come by volition of a people." This was the old Whig dictum of self-determination, taught to Blaine by several of his antebellum mentors. As a young editor in Augusta, Maine, in the 1850s, he had espoused this tenet by advocating Hawaiian annexation with the approval of the native government and the Hawaiian people. When Blaine headed the State Department in the Harrison administration, he changed his stance, at least privately, on the question of overseas territorial expansion. After 1889, he favored taking at least three insular possessions—Hawaii, Cuba, and Puerto Rico—without qualm or concern about the principle of self-determination.[1]

It should be noted that in the case of Hawaii, Secretary Blaine probably thought the self-determination principle was operating. Just before he resigned from the State Department in June 1892, he speculated that American annexation of the Hawaiian Islands was "imminent." The American secretary apparently also believed that such action could be accomplished with the approval of the Hawaiian people because Lorrin A. Thurston, the agent of the Annexation Club who visited Washington that spring, told him a majority of Hawaiians favored annexation. If Blaine accepted Thurston's highly questionable assertion, he was deluded. According to a recent scholar of Hawaiian annexation, Thurston's anticipation that Hawaiians would support annexation was "a preposterous claim." In the early 1890s, residents of Hawaii of American descent or origin, those who were eager for annexation to the United States, made up only 2 percent of the population. The majority of Hawaiians wanted to retain their autonomy and independence as a nation, and many even wished to retain the native monarchy.[2]

Perhaps James G. Blaine's imperial legacy was most apparent in the foreign policy successes of several of his star pupils. Within a decade after his death, two of them, President William McKinley and Secretary of State John Hay, implemented several key features of his blueprints. Both leaders idolized Blaine and acknowledged him as their teacher in the great game of empire. They accepted and acted upon their mentor's call for an American imperium that extended from the Caribbean to Central and South America in the hemisphere and from the Aleutian rim to the Hawaiian and Samoan archipelagos in the Pacific Ocean. For example, the McKinley administration finally resolved the Samoan question in 1899 in an agreement with Germany that partitioned the islands and gave the United States uncontested control of the harbor of Pago Pago. Also, during McKinley's presidency, the U.S. Navy occupied Wake Island as another Pacific stepping-stone to the Far East. The two men followed their mentor's lead on the mainland of Asia as well, where Blaine had been instrumental in pushing open the door in Korea. To be sure, the diplomacy of McKinley and Hay focused on China, but the two men clearly operated on open-door principles similar to those pioneered by Blaine in the Hermit Kingdom. Arguably, it was Blaine who had the defining impact on their imperial thinking and foreign policy.

William McKinley made the annexation of Hawaii one of the top priorities of his presidency. His administration quickly negotiated a new treaty of annexation with representatives of the Hawaiian republic. In June 1897, just three months after McKinley's inauguration, American and Hawaiian officials gathered for the signing ceremony in the State Department's elegant reception room. Lorrin A. Thurston, one of the signers for Hawaii, related in his memoirs that the publisher of the Grand Army of the Republic's official newspaper requested permission to photograph the ceremony for a future issue. Both parties agreed. As they assembled for the photographer, Assistant Secretary Alvey Adee, the institutional memory of the State Department, objected that a portrait of former Secretary of State Walter Q. Gresham, an opponent of annexation, looked down upon the treaty signing. Adee removed the Gresham portrait and speedily replaced it with one of former Secretary James G. Blaine, a leading proponent of Hawaiian annexation. After this symbolic gesture, the signing ceremony was photographed.[3]

In the campaign for Senate ratification of the treaty, President McKinley enlisted the help of another of Blaine's protégés, Senator William P. Frye of Maine. Frye, who had been a key player in the successful fight for renewal of Hawaiian reciprocity in 1887, could not readily duplicate that triumph in behalf of annexation. After months of sustained opposition in the Senate, McKinley, with Frye's aid, ultimately secured approval of the annexation treaty by congressional joint resolution in 1898 during the Spanish-American War. Senator Frye strongly supported McKinley's expansionist policies and, at the conclusion of the victorious war against Spain, was appointed to the peace commission that assembled in Paris. Another former Blaine student and Republican loyalist, Whitelaw Reid of the *New York Tribune*, also was a member of the delegation that negotiated the peace settlement, which brought Puerto Rico, Cuba, and the Philippines into the new American empire. "Taking" Puerto Rico and Cuba in 1898 was well ahead of Blaine's timetable. In 1891 he had written President Harrison that American control of the two Caribbean islands was not "imminent and will not be for a generation." Whether Blaine would have approved of taking the Philippines and suppressing the subsequent Filipino insurrection is problematic, although acquiring those Pacific islands was in line with his designs for American penetration of the Asian continent.[4]

James G. Blaine would have applauded another of the McKinley-Hay team's diplomatic triumphs. Throughout his public career, Blaine had sought to revise the 1850 Clayton-Bulwer Treaty and free the United States to construct and fortify an isthmian canal. As secretary of state under Garfield in 1881, he put the British government on notice that any future interoceanic waterway would have to be American owned and controlled. Shortly after he became head of the State Department, Secretary John Hay began negotiations with the British ambassador, Sir Julian Pauncefote, to terminate the Clayton-Bulwer agreement. The British on this occasion were eager for a rapprochement with the United States and acquiesced to American demands. The 1901 Hay-Pauncefote Treaty settled the long-festering isthmian canal issue by sanctioning the United States' unilateral right to build and fortify a transoceanic waterway and, in turn, opened the way for President Teddy Roosevelt to begin construction of the Panama Canal a few years later.

In addition to his imperial legacies in the Caribbean, Central America, and the Pacific, Blaine also bequeathed his concept of Pan-Americanism to future generations of North and South Americans. This was made clear in the last public address President William McKinley gave before his assassination, when he warmly paid tribute to his mentor at the 1901 Pan-American Exposition in Buffalo, New York. In a speech that brought forth enthusiastic cheers whenever Blaine's name was mentioned, McKinley said: "This exposition would have touched the heart of that American statesman whose mind was ever alert and thought ever constant for a larger commerce and truer fraternity of the republics of the New World. His broad American spirit is felt and manifested here. He needs no identification to an assemblage of Americans anywhere, for the name of Blaine is inseparably associated with the Pan-American movement." Such accolades for Blaine's seminal contribution to Pan-Americanism were echoed throughout the first half of the twentieth century by a number of prominent leaders from the United States and the nations of Latin America.[5]

A few years after McKinley offered homage to Blaine, Elihu Root did the same. Root, who became secretary of state in Theodore Roosevelt's administration after John Hay's death, was a long-time admirer of the Plumed Knight and his Pan-American project. In 1889 Root addressed the delegates to the first Pan-American conference during their visit to New York City, effusively hailing them as "the advance guard in the greatest movement since civilization began towards the brotherhood of man and the federation of the world." Root attended the 1906 Third Inter-American Conference in Rio de Janeiro and was the first secretary of state to travel abroad for such a meeting. After the conference, he embarked on a goodwill tour of South and Central

America that included stops in Argentina, Uruguay, Chile, Peru, Panama, and Colombia. Upon his return, the secretary of state reported on his South American tour at the Trans-Mississippi Commercial Congress in Kansas City, Missouri. He credited Blaine with opening a new era in hemispheric relations and praised his predecessor as a leader "gifted with that imagination which enlarges the historian's understanding of the past into the statesman's comprehension of the future." Secretary Root also told his audience that the time had come to follow "the pathway marked out by the far-sighted statesmanship of Blaine for the growth of America, North and South, in the peaceful prosperity of a mighty commerce."[6]

In the 1920s, the Republican administrations of Warren Harding, Calvin Coolidge, and Herbert Hoover were determined to improve the United States' relations with its hemispheric neighbors. In the first two decades of the twentieth century, the United States frequently had intervened militarily in the internal affairs of the nations of the Caribbean Basin. This "drive to hegemony," as one historian labeled the process, made a mockery of the lofty principles of Pan-Americanism. Hoover, first as secretary of commerce and then as president, wished to end this era of gunboat diplomacy. Immediately after his election victory in 1928, the Iowa Republican of Quaker background visited a number of Latin American countries on a goodwill tour reminiscent of Elihu Root's 1906 journey. During his years in the White House, President Hoover worked to improve Latin American relations and on several occasions praised James G. Blaine as the founder of Pan-Americanism. In that same spirit, on January 31, 1930, the one hundredth anniversary of James G. Blaine's birth, the governing board of the Pan-American Union passed a resolution expressing "gratitude to the memory of the distinguished statesman, Mr. Blaine . . . who was the initiator of the Pan American movement."[7]

The memory of James G. Blaine also was kept alive in the first half of the twentieth century by the persistent efforts of his two surviving daughters, Margaret Blaine Damrosch and Harriet Blaine Beale. When she felt that President Hoover was being inattentive to her father's memory at a Pan-American Day celebration in 1931, Mrs. Damrosch wrote him a chiding letter. A surprised Hoover replied with regret that his failure to mention her father's contributions had caused offense. The Blaine daughters saw the Good Neighbor Policy of Franklin D. Roosevelt and Cordell Hull as the fulfillment of their father's Pan-American vision and were pleased, even though Mr. Republican's policies were being implemented by a Democratic administration. To make sure that James G. Blaine received due recognition in 1940 at the commemoration of the fiftieth anniversary of the founding of the Pan-American Union, Mrs. Beale wrote Secretary of State Hull, reminding him of her father's contributions. Secretary Hull graciously responded "that no one with the slightest interest in the development of American foreign policy can be unmindful of the very valuable service of your father, the Honorable James G. Blaine, in furthering the cause of better and more intimate inter-American relations during the two periods he was Secretary of State." Hull assured Mrs. Beale that her father would be accorded "special recognition" for his achievements at the anniversary commemoration.[8]

One of the last official tributes to James G. Blaine and his Pan-American project occurred in 1943, on the fiftieth anniversary of his death. This elaborate ceremony came at the height of World War II, as the nations of the hemisphere fought for common victory against the Axis powers. It was held at the Pan-American Union Building in Washington, where Luis F. Guachalla, ambassador of Bolivia, opened the ceremony by depositing a wreath at the bust of Secretary Blaine. Three speakers honored Blaine's memory—Undersecretary of State Sumner Welles; Dr. Ricardo J. Alfaro, former president of Panama; and Republican Senator Wallace H. White of Maine. Undersecretary Welles was eloquent and effusive in his tribute: "We mark today the 50th anniversary of the death of James G. Blaine. We undertake this act of commemoration in honor of an American statesman who had a great vision—a vision which we 50 years later see, at least in great part, realized." Welles was confident that "Secretary Blaine would be satisfied with his handiwork if he could today see the outgrowth of the policies which he upheld and of the plans which he initiated."[9]

The other two speakers, Dr. Alfaro and Senator White, were equally expansive in their praise. The former president of Panama commended Blaine as "the man who succeeded in drawing together Anglo-Saxon-America and Latin-America, as the spiritual heir of Simon Bolivar and Henry Clay. . . . No more fitting place could be found for this tribute to James G. Blaine than this stately room" in the Pan-American Building, which was a "monument to his glory" and "the living symbol of the union of twenty-one sovereign republics." For his part, Senator White stressed the economic aspects of Blaine's Pan-American policy, noting that a "basic purpose of this Union has been the promotion of trade between its members." "Mr. Blaine," White continued, "believed in economic understanding between the people of this hemisphere" as the basis for mutual commercial prosperity and political stability. The glowing oratory of Undersecretary Welles, former President Alfaro, and Senator White was music to the ears of the Blaine admirers in the audience, and there could have been no more fitting memorial tribute to Blaine's career.[10]

The name and fame of James G. Blaine are all but forgotten as a new millennium begins. But Blaine of Maine's vision of national greatness and his dream of Pan-Americanism have been realized, and his sense of destiny and mission remain embedded within the concept of American identity. His most enduring legacy is the Organization of American States, created in 1948 as the successor to the Pan-American Union. Among his contemporaries, James G. Blaine was seen as the leading American statesman of his day, the equal of European leaders such as Otto von Bismarck and William E. Gladstone. For succeeding generations of Americans, James G. Blaine should be recognized as an architect of American empire and remembered as one late nineteenth-century leader who truly prepared his nation and its people for what became the American Century.

Notes

1. *New York Tribune,* August 30, 1890.

2. Tom Coffman, *Nation Within: The Story of America's Annexation of the Nation of Hawai'i* (Honolulu: Tom Coffman/Epicenter, 1998), 259–60.

3. Lorrin A. Thurston, *Memoirs of the Hawaiian Revolution* (Honolulu: Advertiser Publishing Co., 1936), 566–67. The GAR newspaper probably was the *Great Republic,* published in Washington, D.C.

4. James G. Blaine to Benjamin Harrison, August 10, 1891, in *The Correspondence Between Benjamin Harrison and James G. Blaine, 1882–1893,* ed. Albert T. Volwiler (Philadelphia: American Philosophical Society, 1940), 174.

5. Alexander K. McClure and Charles Morris, *The Authentic Life of William McKinley* (n.p., 1901), 309–10.

6. Elihu Root quoted in Ricardo J. Alfaro, "A Half Century of Pan Americanism," *Bulletin of the Pan American Union* (April 1940), 228; Root's 1906 speech quoted in *Letters of Mrs. James G. Blaine,* ed. Harriet S. Blaine Beale, 2 vols. (New York: Duffield and Company, 1908), 2:13–14.

7. David Healy, *Drive to Hegemony: The United States in the Caribbean, 1898–1919* (Madison: University of Wisconsin Press, 1988); *Resolution of the governing board of the Pan-American Union,* February 5, 1930, Blaine Papers, Library of Congress.

8. Ibid., Herbert Hoover to Mrs. Margaret Blaine Damrosch, April 20, 1931; Cordell Hull to Mrs. Harriet Blaine Beale, April 1, 1940.

9. Address of the Honorable Sumner Welles, January 27, 1943, Welles Papers, Franklin D. Roosevelt Library, Hyde Park, NY.

10. Addresses of Ricardo J. Alfaro and Wallace H. White, January 27, 1943, Blaine Papers, Library of Congress.

Bibliographical Essay

Scholars of James G. Blaine have adequate, if not abundant, collections of manuscripts and primary materials to examine. The James G. Blaine Papers in the Library of Congress are the most important source for his life and career. The collection includes family papers and correspondence, drafts of Blaine's letters and speeches, State Department dispatches, newspaper clippings and campaign materials, obituaries, and the selected twentieth-century correspondence of his daughters, Margaret Blaine Damrosch and Harriet Blaine Beale, which contains brief appraisals of their father's career as politician and statesman. In addition, there are small collections of Blaine Papers in the Maine Historical Society in Portland and the Maine State Archives in Augusta. The Maine Historical Society also has a small holding of the Papers of John L. Stevens, who was Blaine's newspaper partner and longtime friend. The Whitelaw Reid Papers in the Library of Congress contain the richest source of Blaine correspondence for the 1880s and 1890s. Reid was editor of the *New York Tribune*, a GOP loyalist, and Blaine's political confidante.

Blaine's published works, including speeches in Congress and public addresses, are an indispensable source for understanding his political outlook and position on issues of the day, including foreign and economic policy. The most important are *Twenty Years of Congress: From Lincoln to Garfield* (Norwich, CT, Vol. 1, 1884; Vol. 2, 1886), and *Political Discussions: Legislative, Diplomatic and Popular* (Norwich, CT, 1887). The memorial tribute to the founder of the *Kennebec Journal* and former American commissioner to the kingdom of Hawaii, *Memoir of Luther Severance* (Augusta, 1856), reveals Blaine's early thinking on Hawaiian annexation. Also essential is Blaine's article defending his foreign policy during the brief Garfield presidency, "The South American Policy of the Garfield Administration," *Chicago Weekly Magazine*, September 16, 1882. See as well his eulogy to Garfield in *Memorial Addresses Delivered before the Two Houses of Congress on the Life and Char-*

acter of Abraham Lincoln, James A. Garfield, and William McKinley (Washington, DC, 1903). For an example of Blaine's unbounded faith in the United States' national destiny, see his essay, which was published shortly before his death, "The Progress and Development of the Western World," in *Columbus and Columbia* (Richmond, VA, 1892).

The two-volume published collection, *Letters of Mrs. James G. Blaine* (New York, 1908), edited by Harriet Blaine Beale, is invaluable for its glimpses of Blaine's family life and Mrs. Blaine's lively comments in correspondence to her children on current political and diplomatic events. The miscellaneous and scattered correspondence contained in Gail Hamilton's (Mary Abigail Dodge) *Biography of James G. Blaine* (Norwich, CT, 1895) also is essential to an understanding of the man and his public life. James A. Garfield's candid observations on his friend's character and political style may be found in Theodore Clarke Smith, *The Life and Letters of James Abram Garfield*, 2 vols. (New Haven, CT, 1925). For the Blaine-Harrison relationship, see Albert T. Volwiler, ed., *The Correspondence between Benjamin Harrison and James G. Blaine, 1882–1893* (Philadelphia, 1940). Royal Cortissoz's two-volume *The Life of Whitelaw Reid* (New York, 1921) also contains useful correspondence relating to Blaine's political campaigns and public life. Also helpful for an understanding of Blaine's diplomacy are John Foster's *Diplomatic Memoirs*, 2 vols. (New York, 1909). A revealing essay on Blaine's failed presidential ambitions is Murat Halstead's "The Defeat of Blaine for the Presidency," *McClure's Magazine* (January 1896).

Several newspapers are important for their commentary on Blaine's public career and their coverage of his rise to national prominence as Republican party leader and spokesman, presidential aspirant, and statesman. For Blaine's early years as journalist and editor, the *Kennebec Journal* is an essential reference. The *New York Tribune, New York Times,* and *Chicago Tribune* are the major newspapers to consult for his career in Congress and as national leader. See also two magazines, *Harper's Weekly* and *The Nation,* the latter of which, under E. L. Godkin, was unrelenting in its scathing criticism of Blaine. Media coverage of his 1884 presidential campaign was extensive, and Blaine was mercilessly satirized as "the tattooed man" in the cartoons of *Puck* magazine.

For Blaine's diplomatic career, the files of the State Department are important, as are the published materials of the *Foreign Relations of the United States* series. For his service in the House of Representatives and the Senate, see the *Congressional Globe* and the *Congressional Record.* For his views on reciprocity, see U.S. Senate, *Reciprocity Treaties with the Latin American States,* 51st Cong., 1st sess., 1890 (Washington, DC, 1890). For the proceedings of the first Pan-American conference, see

International American Conference, Reports of Committees and Discussions Thereon, 4 vols. (Washington, DC, 1890). The best full-scale biography of Blaine is David S. Muzzey's *James G. Blaine: A Political Idol of Other Days* (New York, 1935). A more critical, and less reliable, work is Charles Edward Russell's *Blaine of Maine: His Life and Times* (New York, 1931). As a young political correspondent in Washington during the Harrison administration, Russell had observed Blaine firsthand. See also Thomas H. Sherman, *Twenty Years with James G. Blaine* (New York, 1928), an anecdotal and laudatory account by Blaine's longtime secretary. An early popular biography, *James Gillespie Blaine* (Boston, 1905), by Edward Stanwood, a relative of Mrs. Blaine, remains a valuable source.

During the 1884 presidential race a number of campaign biographies appeared, all of which should be used with caution, although Russell H. Conwell's *The Life and Public Service of James G. Blaine* (Hartford, CT, 1884) contains some useful information. The best of the eulogistic works published at the time of Blaine's death is Theron C. Crawford's *James G. Blaine: A Study of His Life and Career* (Philadelphia, 1893). See also Gamaliel Bradford, "James Gillespie Blaine," *Atlantic Monthly* (October, 1920) and the recent, succinct evaluation of Blaine's legislative career by R. Hal Williams, "James G. Blaine," in Donald C. Bacon, Roger H. Davidson, and Morton Keller, eds., *The Encyclopedia of the United States Congress,* 4 vols. (New York, 1995), 1:176–78.

A number of scholarly works offer critical and insightful evaluations of Blaine's foreign policy, including Alice Felt Tyler, *The Foreign Policy of James G. Blaine* (Minneapolis, MN, 1927); David M. Pletcher, *The Awkward Years: American Foreign Relations under Garfield and Arthur* (Columbia, MO, 1963); William Appleman Williams, *The Roots of the Modern American Empire* (New York, 1969); Milton Plesur, *America's Outward Thrust: Approaches to Foreign Affairs, 1865–1890* (DeKalb, IL, 1971); Tom E. Terrill, *The Tariff, Politics, and American Foreign Policy, 1874–1901* (Westport, CT, 1973); Edward P. Crapol, *America for Americans: Economic Nationalism and Anglophobia in the Late Nineteenth Century* (Westport, CT, 1973); Charles S. Campbell, *The Transformation of American Foreign Relations, 1865–1900* (New York, 1976); Robert L. Beisner, *From the Old Diplomacy to the New, 1865–1900* (Arlington Heights, IL, 1975, 1986); Justus D. Doenecke, *The Presidencies of James A. Garfield and Chester A. Arthur* (Lawrence, KS, 1981); Joyce Goldberg, *The Baltimore Affair* (Lincoln, NE, 1986); Homer E. Socolofsky and Allan B. Spetter, *The Presidency of Benjamin Harrison* (Lawrence, KS, 1987); Steven C. Topik, *Trade and Gunboats: The United States and Brazil in the Age of Empire* (Stanford, CA, 1996); and Walter LeFeber's two excellent overviews of the period,

The New Empire: An Interpretation of American Expansion, 1860–1898 (Ithaca, NY, 1963, 1998) and *The American Search for Opportunity, 1865–1913* (New York, 1993). For an admirably concise and perceptive appraisal of Blaine's diplomacy, see Lester D. Langley, "James G. Blaine: The Ideologue as Diplomatist," in Frank J. Merli and Theodore A. Wilson, eds., *Makers of American Diplomacy: From Benjamin Franklin to Alfred Thayer Mahan* (New York, 1974), 253–78.

Index